PRAISE FOR

"This is a wonderful, warm, inspiring book, loaded with great ideas to be happier and healthier in every area of your life."

BRIAN TRACY BESTSELLING AUTHOR OF *MAXIMUM ACHIEVEMENT*, CEO BRIAN TRACY INTERNATIONAL

"Part visual guide and part deeply personal meditation, I kept asking myself, "Why don't they teach this stuff in school?" If every student started their day with these simple exercises, their success would skyrocket."

JOEL COMM FUTURIST, AND *NEW YORK TIMES* BEST-SELLING AUTHOR OF *TWITTER POWER 3.0*

"Easy to read, fun to look at, and highly profound. Bob is a rockstar, and he's done it again!"

JANET BRAY ATTWOOD *NEW YORK TIMES* BESTSELLING AUTHOR OF *THE PASSION TEST*, AND *YOUR HIDDEN RICHES*

"Brilliantly simple and highly profound—the essentials of success in four daily actions. Robert Allen has always been great at simplifying even the most complicated subjects."

DANIEL G. AMEN, M.D. FOUNDER AMEN CLINICS AND AUTHOR OF *CHANGE YOUR BRAIN, CHANGE YOUR LIFE.*

"I love the conversational style: casual but well crafted, direct but not preachy, and totally sincere. I was struck by the book's power and simplicity. Truly love it! Deeply personal and deeply powerful . . . The Four Maps charts a beautifully simple daily practice that will elevate your life by revealing your Hero's Journey. I love this book."

JOHN DAVID MANN COAUTHOR OF THE INTERNATIONAL BESTSELLER, *THE GO-GIVER*

"I can say for sure that The Four Maps is more than just a regular book. It is a clear roadmap that shows you how to live a fulfilled life. If you are aiming high and wish to achieve the incredible, then this book is what you need. It is simple and very powerful, with clear action steps to personal inner growth."

DENIS DOVGAL CEO DOODLEVIDEO.ME

"Robert Allen has reduced success down to 4 simple steps. If you can draw a smiley face and read English this book can help you."

JACK M. ZUFELT AUTHOR OF #1 BESTSELLER, *THE DNA OF SUCCESS*

"Having graduated with a Wharton MBA, I can honestly say they don't they teach this stuff even inside the world's top business schools. I've invested over 34 years of my life studying how the super rich create wealth in America, and Robert Allen is spot on with his insights! Personal growth training is missing from our educational system."

SHERMAN RAGLAND MBA, CCIM, DEAN OF THE REALINVESTORS® ACADEMY AND BESTSELLING AUTHOR OF *AMERICA'S REAL ESTATE MENTOR!"*

"I truly love this book. Action. Action. Action. This book kicked up everything to a new level for me and helped me get unstuck in a few areas of my life. It came at a perfect time!"

ELLE INGALLS PERFORMANCE COACH AND CREATOR OF THE PRESSURE-FREE METHOD AND OPTIMAL PERFORMANCE

"Robert Allen's short, new book will only take you about an hour to devour, but the lessons will reverberate throughout your entire life."

BRIAN WALSH FOUNDER AND CEO OF REAL SUCCESS NETWORK

"When you think about Robert Allen, you think about money. But what is behind all that success? The Four Maps of Happy, Successful People is a must read—give it to everybody you love. A great life lesson from a giant thinker."

ALFIO BARDOLLA BESTSELLING AUTHOR, *MONEY MAKES YOU HAPPY*, AND *BUSINESS REVOLUTION*

"What a rich gift to the world! This book is powerful and life changing. It pricked my conscience and spoke to my soul. I loved it!"

JUDGE GLENDA HATCHETT STAR OF THE AWARD WINNING SHOW, *JUDGE HATCHETT* AND AUTHOR OF *DARE TO TAKE CHARGE: HOW TO LIVE YOUR LIFE ON PURPOSE*

LittleBetter Books
Los Angeles, CA

ISBN: 978-0-9971033-1-1

Cover and interior design by Martin Rock.
Drawings by Denis Dovgal and Doodlevideo.me.

This publication contains opinions designed to help and motivate its readers. It is sold with the understanding that these opinions are for education purposes only, and that the authors and publisher are not offering any type of professional advice, whether psychological, legal, or financial. Every effort has been made to make this book as accurate as possible. However, there may be errors, and by no means is this book designed to be an exhaustive source on the topics discussed. The publisher and the authors assume no responsibility for any errors, inaccuracies, or omissions. We wish you the best, but only you are responsible for your choices, actions, and results.

littlebetterbooks.com

THE FOUR MAPS OF HAPPY SUCCESSFUL PEOPLE

THE FOUR MAPS OF HAPPY SUCCESSFUL PEOPLE

by

ROBERT G. ALLEN

with

AARON ALLEN

littleBETTER

Los Angeles | California

FREE QUICKSTART BUNDLE

I want to say thanks for purchasing the *Four Maps of Happy Successful People*. I know there's a reason you picked up this book. I want to do everything possible to help you succeed. I've created a Free Four Maps QuickStart Guide full of printable tips, checklists, and images. It's designed to help you get the most out of what you are about to read. Visit the website below to immediately access your QuickStart Guide.

WWW.ROBERTALLEN.COM/QUICKSTART

CONTENTS

PART ONE:
THE DRAWING BOARD

INTRODUCTION

IN THIS BOOK I've outlined how you can dramatically improve your life by drawing four diagrams every day. The diagrams are very simple—stick figures mostly—and can easily be drawn by almost anyone. I call these diagrams the Four Maps because... well...they look like maps. ☺ They are personalized maps of your journey to an ideal lifestyle—whatever you decide that means for you.

The Four Maps aren't an instant miracle or magic-bullet cure to make you happy and successful—they are designed to work over time in your life and are backed up by the latest neuroscience. The goal is to change your brain and your behavior day by day until you consistently adopt the outlook, attitudes, habits, and task management strategies of the world's most successful, most efficient people. Once you develop those attributes, success will follow in whatever fields you choose.

All that might be hard to believe, but I've been teaching these Four Maps, or versions of them, for over twenty years, to thousands of clients and students—from huge corporations, to startup incubators, to working professionals, to athletes, to artists and writers, to my own children—and I've seen them change lives first-hand. I know they can work for you—if you put them to work.

Have you ever had a moment of perfect clarity? You knew exactly what you wanted, why you wanted it, and what you needed to do, right in that moment, in order to get it. Moments of clarity can come from reading a book, facing the turn of the calendar, being in nature, sitting in church, watching a thoughtful movie, meditating, being with the people you love, (or seeing them pass on), among many other things. When we are in a moment of clarity, we can see the "big picture," and are more likely to adopt productive attitudes and take effective action towards big picture goals (as opposed to wasting time and energy on things that end up meaning very little).

The secret of long-term behavioral change is to be in that big picture state of mind as much as possible—not just once each year with New Year's Resolutions, not only when the sunset falls just right behind the sea, and not just when we look into the eyes of a newborn.

The problem is that our brains are "forgetting machines." One moment we can be totally clear on what we want, why we want it, and exactly how to get it, and the next moment we forget completely and slip back into our old unproductive routines and thought processes.

If this has ever happened to you, don't be too hard on yourself—it's just a part of being human. The latest neuroscience (plus a lot of common sense) shows that our brains really, really don't like change. They like to keep doing things the way they've always done them. If we try to change, our brains try to rebound back to old behaviors and thought patterns. They boomerang. If you're reading this book (and you're human), it's likely that your normal thought patterns often lead you to procrastinate, fail to reach goals, lack direction and clarity, feel overwhelmed, overstressed, and lost in chaos.

Or maybe you've taken care of the mindset aspects of your life, but are still struggling with choosing effective actions to maximize your time. Whatever your situation, I repeat, please don't be too hard on yourself. Even nature loves chaos. The second law of thermodynamics calls it entropy—the tendency of the universe to move towards the path of least resistance.

But what makes us human (and amazing) is our desire to keep improving, determined that we can change. And there are some people who seem to be "on top of things"—hyper-achievers. How do we become one of them? How do we change a brain that is a forgetting machine?

The answer is simple but very deep: We can't really stop our brains from being long-term forgetting machines—it's something we just have to accept and live with—but we *can* overcome the problem by turning on a daily "reminding machine." We can keep telling our brains, in powerful ways, exactly how we want them to think, to view the world, and to approach and overcome challenges. The most successful people in the world have the same brains as everyone else, but they choose to be in control. They don't let their forgetting machines determine how they view situations—they tell their brains how to react to the world, and they do it as part of a routine, every single day.

Think of your brain as a stubborn mule (but one that you love deeply ☺). In order to get the mule to work hard, do you tell it just once, on January 1st, what you want it to do? How would that end up? How quickly would the mule, stubborn as it is, fall back into its favorite behaviors? The way to work with a stubborn mule is to keep reminding it every day (and sometimes multiple times a day) what you expect from it.

Most success philosophies (and self-improvement books) contain wonderful, helpful information but fail to change behavior in the long run because they don't focus on making their message a daily practice. The modern world is crazy busy, and we don't have time to read an entire book each morning to get in the right frame of mind. I believe we need a system that, in ten minutes or so, helps us find the big picture.

That's exactly what the Four Maps accomplish. They are daily reminding machines. And you will customize them so that they become personal to your own life, and enormously powerful.

There are so many other analogies I could use to describe what the Four Maps are designed to do for you. They recharge your batteries so you have enough energy and belief to go out and win your day. They are a workout for your brain, so you remember what's really important and can focus on getting it done. They are a spring-cleaning to tidy up your mind and clear away the thousands of distractions of modern life, so you can spend your energy on what really matters.

Everything in this book—from the diagrams to the chapter structure, to even the way the sentences are written—is designed to help you transform. The Maps themselves are very simple and easy to draw. In places, the book is also extremely simple, almost comically simple. I'm warning you right now that this is a different kind of book—designed so that even a child could read and understand it. As we go along, I'll touch briefly on the psychology and neuroscience behind the Four Maps, but I won't always go deep into the evidence. My main goal is to help you take action, not just *take in* information. I've included a reading list at the end of the book if you are research-oriented and want to dive deep into the science behind the Four Maps.

In places, this is also a very direct book, and I hope my directness doesn't come across as smug, or all-knowing. I hope my sense of humor and personality will have a chance to squeak through, as well as my genuine desire that this book reaches you.

The vast majority of the people I meet are *so very close* to achieving their dreams, whatever they might be. And I feel a sense of urgency to help. I turned 68 this year! I can hardly believe it. Time really does fly. At my age the priorities are crystal clear: Share what I've learned in the simplest, most effective way possible. Ignore almost everything else ☺ .

I'm not a psychologist, but I have dedicated my life to teaching success principles. Through my various books and businesses I've been "life-hacking," "TED-talking," and "thought-leading" since long before those concepts had names.

The Four Maps are in many ways my "last lesson." Everything I've learned about success is in these pages. If I only had once chance to help you, I would teach you these Four Maps.

In case you are a left-brained person who absolutely needs to know the fine print ☺, I'll touch briefly on the concepts behind Four Maps. The basic idea is that pictures are better than words when it comes to learning, memory, motivation, and personal transformation. The scientific term for this is the Picture Superiority Effect. What we see and draw has a far greater impact on our brains than what we read or write. Instead of just writing down affirmations, or goals, or mantras, the Four Maps are designed to help you draw your future ideal lifestyle. They are visual mnemonic devices, and they are engineered to help you adopt the mindsets, habits, neuroplasticity, reactions, and expectations common to successful individuals. Everything in the drawings is supported by scientific research, thousands of years of cultural proof, and my own lifetime of observations from the front lines of personal development training.

Although the pictures remain simple, there are dozens of positive behavioral science principles at work behind the scenes. As you learn the drawings and make them a daily habit in your life, those dozens of principles will become permanent aspects of your character. The Four Maps also serve as easy ways of presenting, remembering, and quickly recalling massive amounts of information. It would take books and books for me to explain the multitude of strategies at work when you learn and draw one of the Four Maps.

Of course, another way of saying all that is, “a picture is worth a thousand words” ☺ .

A picture is also worth a new start in life, or a new push towards a life goal. There is magic in the Four Maps. I believe they can help you clarify your purpose—the reason you were put on earth. I believe they can help you find your motivations and make you a far more efficient human being. I’ve seen so many of my clients and students brighten after drawing the Four Maps. I believe they can make you happier. I can’t wait to share them with you.

GUIDING PRINCIPLES

THERE ARE THREE principles I want you to keep in mind as we draw the Four Maps together. Think of them as guiding truths that influence everything we're going to talk about. You'll find versions of these principles wherever you look—they are scattered across literature and every self-improvement book ever written. Versions of these truths are part of most major religions and spiritual practices. You might be nodding along in agreement as you read them, or you might have to trust me at first. I'll only touch on them briefly, but the science and human history behind them could fill book after book.

PRINCIPLE 1: SUCCESS IS INSIDE OUT

Success starts inside, whatever you are trying to accomplish, and then manifests in the outside world.

There are zero long-term exceptions to this rule. The happiest, most successful people take care of their internal world before they go out to conquer the external one.

When I was 30 and still a young pup, I wrote a #1 *New York Times* bestseller about investing in real estate. Then I spent years teaching financial investment strategies and writing finance-based books. The stories I could tell you about that crazy world!

I'm proud of my past, but I came to realize that if my clients and readers didn't have the right mentality, they would have a much harder time successfully implementing my strategies. They wouldn't be able to overcome discouragement or rejection (all huge parts of business and entrepreneurship), and they would eventually lose focus and give up. "Inner wealth" had to happen before "outer wealth" could manifest.

I learned the importance of inner wealth from my students, but I also learned first-hand. I've definitely seen some ups and downs in my life. No one is immune to challenges. I've made great decisions and really, really bad ones. I've made and lost fortunes. I can trace every single one of my bad decisions back to a loss of clarity in the moment I made the decision. My internal world wasn't in order. I didn't have a clear picture of my immediate and long-term aspirations, and I was unprepared for the challenges I was facing.

On the other hand, when I matched real-world action with the right mindset, I was unstoppable—and you will be too.

I designed the Four Maps to work inside-out in your life. The first two maps are "internal"—to help you get clear on what you want, and why you want it. They are mindset-based. The last two maps are "external"—they deal with the specific, real-world tasks needed to reach your ideal lifestyle. They are action-based.

Here are the names of the Four Maps:

Internal:

1. Clarity
2. Anticipation

External:

3. Ritual
4. Task

Success starts inside, but we live in a world that demands real, measurable progress. Mindset and attitude are the foundations, and then you build on them with effective, daily action.

PRINCIPLE 2: THE EXPIRATION DATE ON ANY COMMITMENT IS 24 HOURS

At least once a day we have to recommit powerfully to our personal vision.

We've already talked about our brains as forgetting machines. They are hardwired for the moment, which is why it's so difficult to say no to immediate rewards (like ice-cream) even when they might hurt a long-term commitment (like losing weight). The ice cream is right there, and it looks so good. The world around us also seems designed to make us forget the commitments we make. All day we're bombarded with thousands of messages—from the ding of an email notification, or the whisper of a critical thought, to the carefully crafted persuasion of an advertisement. Each of those messages can entice us away from the things that have true value. The only way to overcome distraction is to remind ourselves constantly of our worthy commitments.

I don't mean to say that everything we see around us is a negative distraction. There are often things we need to pay attention to—beautiful sights, wonderful opportunities and inspirational positive messages (like this book ☺). But, in order to separate the distractions from the inspirations, we need a clear, committed vision. And we need to keep reminding ourselves of it—daily.

I hope you will find the Four Maps valuable, and want to draw them every day, although just once will still have a positive effect on your life. In addition, at the end of each of the Four Maps, I'm going to ask you to sign your name and make a 24-hour commitment with yourself.

PRINCIPLE 3: EVERY DECISION YOU MAKE IS BASED ON EITHER A DREAM OR A FEAR

I like to think of a human as a machine running two software programs simultaneously. There is the fear program urging us to make decisions based on selfish immediate needs—on the bad experiences of our past, on our worries for our future, on our lack of self-belief, on all our combined anxieties. And then there is the dream program that is urging us to make decisions based on our goals for the future—on our positive vision for ourselves, on our love for others, and our hope for the human race.

Fears and dreams are in direct competition. Each of them is trying to become the reason for our actions. When you make a decision, any decision, it will be based either on a dream or on a fear. It's the famous image of the good angel on one shoulder and the bad angel on the other. Dream-based decisions are based on principles of abundance. They move you closer to your best self. They make you a more positive person and a kinder, wiser person. I like to think of dream-decisions as ones that enlarge your influence and your impact on the world. Fear-based decisions make you small—they stunt your personal growth and lead to selfishness, pettiness, anxiety, and frustration.

Sadly, most of us are running fear software as our default mindset. In fact, many neuroscientists believe that the brain is evolutionarily hardwired to be fear-based. So, we have to work to be dream-based and make dream-based decisions. It's not something that is going to come without effort. I'm not talking about blind optimism and rose-colored glasses. I'm talking about *choosing* to be hopeful and determined. I've been saying it for over twenty years, and it's still true: every day you must make your dreams more real than your fears.

The most powerful way to make your dreams more real than your fears is to vividly imagine your dreams, as if they had already happened. Research has shown that visualization is a key to success in almost every endeavor—from sports to business to relationships. There is a place in each of the Four Maps for you to take a moment and visualize. In fact, one of the main reasons I designed the Four Maps to be a daily practice was to create a visualization habit in your life—to help you make your dreams more real than your fears.

DIVE IN

A final note before we begin drawing. This book is going to teach you a way to organize your time and your life through the Four Maps. I know there are other systems out there that do similar things, with different advice, and different metaphors. I think they are wonderful! Humanity is endlessly creative, and there are thousands of success systems out there.

You might not resonate with what I'm teaching, but even if the Four Maps don't speak to you, I urge you to find a system that you love, dive into it, and make it a daily practice.

Most people spend far too much time searching for a system, and not nearly enough time working within one. I'm sure you've heard the term *Carpe Diem*, "seize the day." I believe in *Carpe System*. Find a system that you love, that works for you, dive in, and don't let go. Choose a system, and then master it!

PART TWO:
THE FOUR MAPS

MAP 1 CLARITY

HOW TO CREATE A PERSONAL VISION AND NEVER LOSE SIGHT OF IT AGAIN

THE FIRST of the Four Maps is all about your inner life and belief system. It's designed to give you perfect clarity. What is clarity? Clarity is knowing exactly what you want and exactly why you want it. Another word for clarity is "purpose." When we're done with the Clarity Map, you'll have a personalized vision for your future, you'll know *why* you want that future, and you'll know *where* to put your energy to make it a reality.

You'd be shocked how few people actually know what they want. Most of humanity settles for short term, materialistic goals, or moves crisis to crisis through life, grasping at what they think they need, but never focusing their energy towards specific, targeted outcomes. You'd be shocked at how few people are actually "on purpose"—committed and working towards their dreams. But greatness is possible! I believe that greatness is within the reach of any concentrated, targeted, effort. I believe that consistent effort over time will always lead to success.

Before I begin each day, I take the immediate action of finding my clarity, of powerfully remembering, reconnecting, and recommitting to my dreams. Here's how I do it:

Take out a piece of blank paper and a pen, or your favorite digital device. In the top left hand corner of the page write the word "Clarity"—this is your Clarity Map after all. And in the bottom left hand corner of the blank page draw a frowny face.

I know, I know. It feels silly. You're an educated person. Too smart for this kindergarten stuff.

I warned you that this book is different. Just play along for a little longer. Remember, the best way to grow is to do.

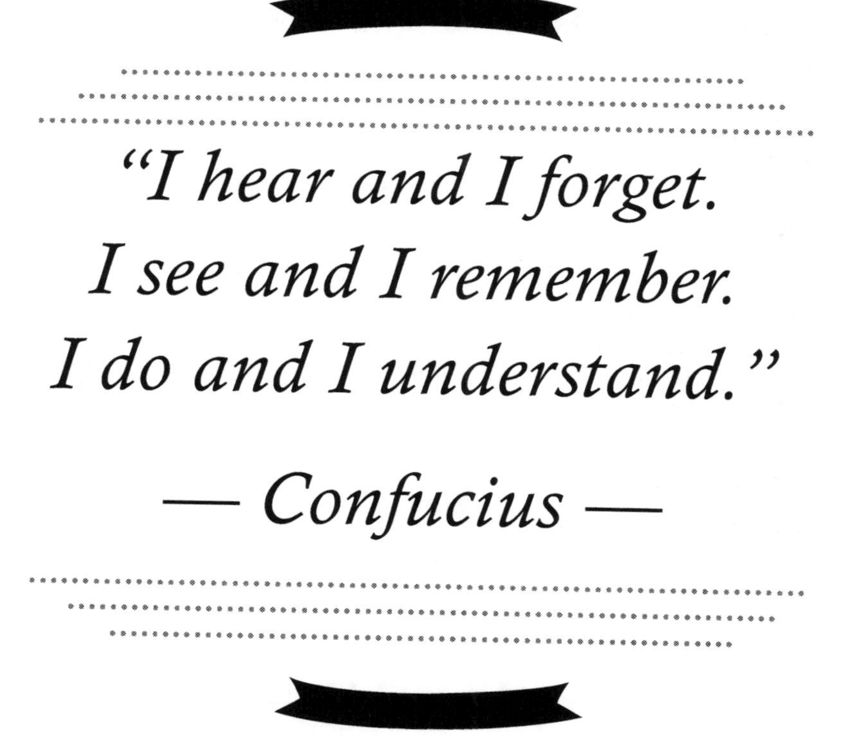
"I hear and I forget.
I see and I remember.
I do and I understand."
— Confucius —

So try it—draw a frowny face in the lower left corner. Maybe you hesitate because your drawing skills are a little rusty. I won't ask you to draw anything too difficult. Anyone can draw a frowny face.

Now, in the upper right hand corner, draw a smiley face. At this point, your picture might be looking something like this:

CLARITY

There should be two images on the page. A frowny face (lower left) and a smiley face (upper right) Got it? I'll be providing an example for everything we draw together, so don't get overwhelmed if you don't grasp how to draw something from the text alone.

That frowny face represents how life feels without clarity. In fact, I want you to draw a square around that frowny face. Now the frowny face is trapped inside a box. This represents the limitations of not knowing what you want. When you don't have clarity in your life you are effectively trapped, held hostage by your own fears, or by the fears and needs of others. It's a short trip from feeling trapped to feeling overwhelmed. Overwhelmed with too many things to do and too little time to do them. Overstrained with relationships that don't work. Overstressed with declining health issues. Overburdened with money pressures. You become an agent to someone else's clarity and vision, and end up working for their purpose, not your own.

Now I want you to look closely at your smiley face. He or she is on top of the mountain, living an Ideal Lifestyle.

That's an interesting concept: "Ideal Lifestyle," and it's one we're going to use often in the Four Maps. So let's stop just a second to think about it.

What does "Idea Lifestyle" mean to you? Top of the heap? Crème de la crème? If you could create an Ideal Lifestyle, what would it look like? Externally, where would you be? Would you be living where you are now? Would you be on a boat in Tahiti? What would you be doing with your time? What would your inner life look like? More patience with family and friends? More compassion? Would your life resemble the one you live now?

Over years of teaching and thousands of students, I've come to believe there are four key elements to every Ideal Lifestyle.

1. Loving relationships: An Ideal Lifestyle is full of rewarding relationships with friends and family that you love and respect.

2. Health: An Ideal Lifestyle is a healthy lifestyle, both spiritually and physically. If you don't have health, nothing else matters.

3. Time freedom: An Ideal Lifestyle is one where you have the time available to get done all that you want to do.

4. Financial freedom: An Ideal Lifestyle is free from debt, and earns enough for you to save and invest while living where you want and being able to help others.

Sound about right? Let's draw the elements of an Ideal Lifestyle on our Clarity Map. Draw another box, this time around the smiley face. Except I want you to make this box a house by putting a roof on top and a door in the front. (Examples are coming up.) This is your dream home. It's a representation of your Ideal Lifestyle. Inside the dream home, let's draw four symbols. Draw a heart to represent a life full of loving relationships, a money ($) sign to represent financial freedom, a clock to represent time freedom, and a stick figure body to represent health. Here is what a dream home looks like ☺:

CLARITY

YOU'RE ON THE PATH

Look closely at the two faces. This is the way many people view their lives. The frowny face represents where they are now—their "before" story. The smiley face, surrounded by the markers of the Ideal Lifestyle, represents where they'd like to be—their "after" story. This book is about getting you to that "after" story. And it's a journey—we're going up a mountain. I want you to draw a line on your Clarity Map connecting the frowny face in its limiting box to the smiley face in its dream home. It should look something like this:

Now it's a true mountain, complete with a path to the top. The Four Maps all use the metaphor of climbing a mountain. You'll literally be drawing the image of your personal mountain and your personal journey.

Just as there are different stages to successfully climbing a mountain, from planning and preparing, to "putting boots on the ground" and summiting, there are essential stages to every successful life.

Each of the Four Maps is going to begin by drawing this exact picture of the two faces, the box and house, and the slope up the mountain. Once you have understood these few simple shapes, the drawing is going to be easy, and the sections are going to be much shorter.

You might feel that you have many aspects of your Ideal Lifestyle already in place. In that case, your journey is going to be about going after the few things you lack. There is a fine line between loving your life, accepting and enjoying what you have, while also continuing to strive towards worthwhile goals. As we talk about this journey to your Ideal Lifestyle, I don't want you to forget about the ways you are already successful. But I also don't want you to get complacent. In my experience, successful people are always striving. There is something they are always stretching towards.

WHAT DO YOU WANT?

Back on your Clarity Map, draw a plus sign (+) in the middle-top part of the page, with three (3) blank lines below it.

Now draw a minus sign (-) on the left side of the page, directly above the frowning face. Put another three (3) blank lines below the (-). It should look like this:

Imagine you have a magic wand and, with a simple wave of the wand, you are living your Ideal Lifestyle. What things have you added to your life? In the blank lines below the (+) sign, write down the three (3) things that come most powerfully to mind. Hopefully I've gotten you thinking about a few of these things as you've been reading. These are things that you wanted, desperately. When they became part of your Ideal Lifestyle you were incredibly happy. They can be material possessions, like a new home, but try to think deeper than that. What do you really, really want? I'll share an exercise that might help you discover what you want, though you certainly shouldn't go through it every time you draw your Clarity Map. If you already know exactly what you want, feel free to skip ahead.

THE "WHAT DO YOU WANT?" GAME

The "what do you want?" game has been around a long time, and it's a powerful tool for building trusting relationships. It's also great for finding clarity. There are many variations, but it goes something like this:

Get comfortable with someone you love and trust (or someone you're ready to love and trust). One person is the asker—the other person is the answerer. Try it first without eye contact, because it can get pretty intense. The asker asks the single question, "what do you want?" in a neutral tone. The answerer responds with the first thing that comes to mind. It can be anything. It can be popcorn. In fact, it usually is something very silly right at first. When the answerer is done saying what he or she wants, the asker repeats the question, "what do you want?" and the answerer once again says the first thing that comes to mind. Do this for anywhere from five to twenty minutes, and then switch sides.

Yup...the same question...the whole time.

It's very important that the asker never says anything other than "what do you want?," in a neutral tone. This is a game where there is absolutely no judgment. There's not even any extended discussion. You can talk about issues that arise later. The goal is to create free association for the answerer, so that everyone feels comfortable and willing to say what comes first to mind.

What ends up happening is, after the first few answers, the mind clears, and the answerer starts getting to the heart of what he or she really wants. Sometimes the question is asked a hundred times before clarity comes. There are silly answers, and general answers (like world peace, or more money) but by the end, the answerer is usually getting specific about deeply felt wants and needs, as well as the reasons that drive all those needs. The effect can be almost magical if the two people trust each other.

So, what do you want for your future? To overcome your issues with self-confidence? To start a business so that you can leave your job? To fit into your high-school jeans? To repair a failed relationship? To fill your life with love? To start a foundation? What do you really want?

WRITE DOWN WHAT YOU WANT

Go back to your Clarity Map and, if you haven't already, write down three (3) of your "wants" below the (+) sign. These wants lead directly to your Ideal Lifestyle! Your Ideal Lifestyle is achievable. Make enough of your wants reality, and you'll be there.

Did you do it? Or did you read ahead quickly to see where this is going? ☺

If you actually did it...well done! Reach your hand over your shoulder and pat yourself on the back.

If you didn't do it, remember, this is a "doing book" as much it is a "learning book." So start doing! Think of those three (3) wants and write them down! The odds of getting the things you want go up dramatically when you write them down.

Good. Now, imagine that with a simple wave of your wand you could improve your life by instantly subtracting (-) three (3) negative things from it.

Ask yourself, "What could I subtract from my life now to make it more ideal?" In the spaces below the (-) sign, write down three (3) things you would remove or eliminate from your life. I call these negative things "don't-wants." Pretty obvious ☺. You shouldn't have to think long to come up with your don't-wants. It's a sad reality that we often think about the negative aspects of our lives—our fears—far more than we think about our ideals and dreams. One of the purposes of the Clarity Map is to give you a workout in flipping that thought process.

That should rev up your imagination—thinking about what you want (+) and don't want (-). Again, here's what your Clarity Map might look like now, except that you will

have all those lines filled in with wants and don't-wants: But *why* do you want what you want? In order to reach the summit of your Ideal Lifestyle, you have to have powerful motivating reasons. Let's dive in and draw your reasons.

YOUR REASONS ARE YOUR ENGINES

Take a moment to ponder why you are motivated to make this difficult journey up your personal mountain. In the open space below the dream house, add the word "Why" and draw three (3) blank lines below it. It should look something like this:

We all have reasons behind the decisions we make. If we don't have a reason for doing something, we don't do it. Simple as that. Our reasons are our motivations for action.

But not all reasons are created equally. If we have bad reasons, we will have less motivation to act. If we have great reasons, we'll be unstoppable.

I like to think of our reasons as engines, pushing us up the mountain towards our Ideal Lifestyle. And not all engines are the same. Some engines are short-term, high-power machines. They are good for giving you a quick burst but are really bad when it comes to staying power. Others are slow-burners, providing a small amount of thrust over a long period of time.

It's the same with our reasons. The better the reason, the better the engine. Choose a short-term reason for going after your wants and you'll inevitably plateau, stall, and fall back. Choose only a long-term reason and you might never even have the energy to start! What the world calls "procrastination," I call "bad reasons." If you have a clear "why," nothing will stop you.

Here's the good news: You're in control of choosing your reasons. Just like your dreams, you're the boss. But you can't choose the right reasons unless you know what they are. So, what are the types of reasons?

There have been hundreds of studies and books dedicated to identifying the motivators behind human behavior. The Bob Allen condensed version is that our reasons fall into three categories, and each one is a different type of engine, with unique motivating power: Need, Me, and We Reasons.

NEED REASONS

Need Reasons are your short-term, high-power, motivators. If you are starving, then you need food, and you are willing to do anything to get it. You'd walk twenty miles if there were food waiting at the end. If you are bankrupt, you need money. You're motivated to work eighty hours a week. If the man or woman you love, the man or woman you *need* ☺ , tells you that he or she will move out unless you bike across America, then chances are you are getting on that bike. Need Reasons are incredibly powerful.

But here's the thing about needs: they get met! If you work hard enough with a Need Reason as your motivation, the need will eventually be taken care of. And what happens then to the motivation? If a starving person gets food, their Need Reason disappears completely, and they aren't motivated to keep looking for food until hunger comes up again. What about someone who is earning good money at a job but aspires for so much more? They feel stuck. They feel they have plateaued personally. Their basic needs are met, (they have a job) and therefore a need engine is not going to help them make the breakthrough. They are going to need a different class of reason.

ME REASONS

When you looked up to the sky as a child what did you want for yourself? To become an astronaut? A fireman? An athlete? An opera singer? As far back as I can remember I wanted to be a millionaire. I grew up middle class in a small town in Alberta, Canada, and the word "millionaire" had such sheen to it for a small-town boy. And that fascination stayed with me my entire young life. I remember going to see my fiancée's mother, my future mother-in-law, a few weeks before I proposed. I guess I was there so she could "check me out" and see if I was good enough for her daughter. She looked me right in the eye and asked me what I was going to do with my life. I looked right back and told her I was going to be a millionaire. I chuckle and cringe a bit remembering that story now, mostly because "millionaire" was such an arbitrary thing to wish for, and because of how brash I was with my mother-in-law...(and she could hardly wait to share this "questionable news" with her daughter! ☺) but nothing was going to stop me from getting that first million.

If I were to dig deeper into my psyche, I would say that my millionaire need was driven by my desire to overcome my humble beginnings—to prove that I could make something of my life. Back then I was very finance-focused, and I thought that making a million dollars was proof that I had made it.

My millionaire reason was a Me Reason. I didn't want the money to fill an urgent need, and I didn't want the money to help others. I wanted the money because of something inside myself.

Can you think of other Me Reasons? Often our reasons for losing weight are Me Reasons—so we can look good in jeans at our high school reunions. Often our reasons for athletic success are Me Reasons—so we can finish first in the race, or outrun all tacklers.

Me Reasons are good long-term engines. They are powerful and they help push you up the mountain, especially when you are young and eager to prove yourself. But there is a type of reason exponentially more powerful...

WE REASONS

We Reasons are by far the most powerful motivator of human behavior, but also the most difficult to clarify in our lives. Any desire to help someone else is a We Reason. But so many of us have vague desires to help others. *Sure I'd like to start a foundation and give back*, we might think, *but I can't see how that is the most powerful motivating engine. In fact, I don't know if I care about others enough to act*. I've been there. But I'm here to tell you that We Reasons are incredible. They are perpetual power plants of motivation.

The secret to making a We Reason a bulletproof motivator is doing it for someone you love. Yup, love is the answer. Case in point:

A woman I mentored once told me she wanted to be a millionaire. I asked her why? She said her son was disabled and the government program that supported his needs was being eliminated. She needed to make enough money or he would die. She was motivated! And nothing was going to deter her. See the difference in power between her We Reason and a self-centered Me Reason?

We Reasons are so powerful that we often refer to them as the purpose of our lives. You've heard that before, right? The purpose of your life. When you have a We Reason so strong that you are willing to label it the very purpose of your existence, then you have endless motivation. And endless motivation is definitely our goal. We're heading to our Ideal Lifestyle, which is also the world's Ideal Lifestyle, full of happy, healthy

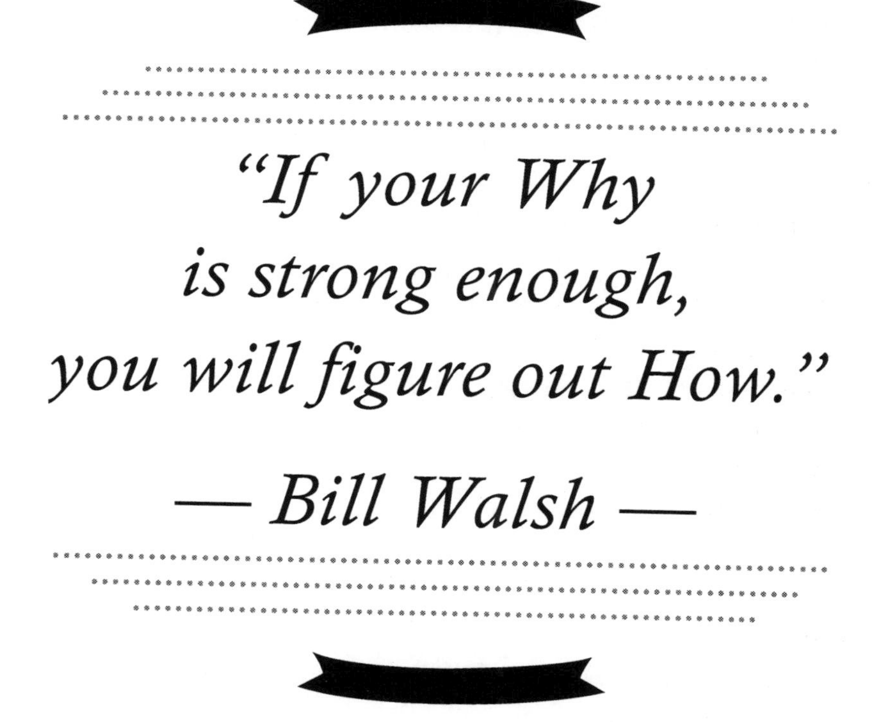
"If your Why
is strong enough,
you will figure out How."
— Bill Walsh —

"The two most important days in your life are the day you are born and the day you find out why."

— Mark Twain —

people. It's going to take a lot of work to get there. We need the best reason engines we can find.

I know it sounds corny, and you might not be in a place yet where you can agree with me, but love really is the answer. Increase the amount of love you have for others, clarify that love every day, and you will never run out of energy or motivation. In other words: you will never procrastinate again.

WRITE DOWN YOUR REASONS

Have you been thinking of your reasons? If not, take some time now to do so. Then go back to your Clarity Map and write down three (3) of your most powerful reasons on the lines next to "Why?"

USE ALL TYPES OF REASONS

It's perfectly fine to mix and match Need, Me, and We Reasons as you write down your three (3). It's also perfectly fine now if you don't have any We Reasons. Incredible things have been accomplished with Need and Me Reasons only. You'll find your We Reasons in time if you haven't yet. I didn't define my purpose in life until I was well into my forties.

If you think about the symbols in your dream home—your markers of an Ideal Lifestyle—you'll find that each of them can be motivated by all three (3) of the reason engines. You might *need* money to pay off pressing debt, want money *for yourself* to build a dream home, and want money *for others* to alleviate suffering, all at the same time. Or take health, for example. You might be a diabetic and *need* to exercise to get your blood sugar under control, want to exercise *for yourself* to compete in a 5k you've had your eye on, and want to found a children's lunch initiative so *others* can get healthy, sugar-free meals. You'll be able to find a reason for each and every one of your wants. Find that reason now, and write it down.

FEEL THE IDEAL

Okay, so let's recap. Now we know what we want. We've written down three (3) of our wants (+), and we've written down three (3) things we'd like to eliminate from our lives (-). We know that reasons are our engines to help push us towards our Ideal Lifestyle. We've written down our personalized reasons. Are you feeling charged up yet? Are you feeling clear? Is your personalized vision starting to form?

There's only one thing left to do on our Clarity Map, and that's to make it real.

This is also the most important step. Most of what you've just written down is not going to change much day-to-day. Once you fill it out this first time, you'll probably keep the same reasons, wants and don't-wants. So, why do the Clarity Map every day?

Because it's not enough just to think lightly of our Ideal Lifestyle, or to have a simple list of what we want. To get the full benefits we have to make it real. In the guiding principles section I talked about the power of visualization to make your dreams more real than your fears. I like to take it one step further and "virtualize" aspects of my Ideal Lifestyle. I try to experience it—feel it—as if I was virtually living it.

I enjoy drawing my Four Maps everyday, but my experience with them often goes deeper than enjoyment. It's a form of personal meditation. As I'm drawing each element of my Clarity Map I'm pausing, closing my eyes, and trying to vividly imagine what I'm writing. I never finish my map without this powerful step. Virtualization is what gives the Four Maps their power to change your life—it helps transform simple daily doodles into profound images.

Maybe you've been virtualizing as you've read along, and maybe your Clarity Map already feels real to you. But, in case you haven't, now is the time to do it.

There are two key spots where I take extra time to stop and virtualize. The first happens as I imagine what my Ideal Lifestyle will be like.

I want you to experience your Ideal Lifestyle with all five senses each time you draw your smiley face in your dream home. Smell, taste, feel, hear, and see aspects of your success as if you were actually living it right now. This is what it means to virtualize.

How would your life feel if it was full of loving relationships? How would it feel to be financially free? What would you do with your time? Would you sail across the world? If so, what would that feel like? Try to inhabit the exhilaration of rushing on a wave. Try to feel the wind on your face. What a great life. Try to see, hear, and smell all of your Ideal Lifestyle. Feel it in present tense…as if it were happening right now. Try to feel the ideal.

The second place where I like to virtualize my Clarity Map is when I think of my reasons. When you virtualize your reasons, try to imagine the people you love benefiting from your effort. How will they feel when you accomplish your Ideal Lifestyle? Try to see the smiles on their faces and the gratitude in their eyes. Or imagine how great it's going to feel when you finish first and accomplish one of your Me Reasons. If you have a desperate need, try to imagine what your life will be like when that need is met. Try to make it real. The more vivid you can make your virtualization, the more motivating power it will provide you throughout the day. Remember, humans are forgetting machines. We're always losing sight of what's really important. When we virtualize our Ideal Lifestyle, and our reasons for getting there, it becomes very hard to forget and get off track in the 24 hours before we re-commit.

Did you do it? Did you virtualize your Clarity Map? Give yourself a big pat on the back. Virtualization is the way we make our dreams more real than our fears, everyday.

I want you to go back to your Clarity Map and write, "Feel the Ideal" on the slope going up the mountain. It's there to remind you that you have to virtualize your clarity, every day. It should look like this:

MAKE THE COMMITMENT

The only thing missing from your Clarity Map is your signature—your 24-hour Commitment. Put a line for the date and a line for your signature in the bottom right hand corner, like this:

Stop for a second before you make this commitment. Take a deep breath. Are you ready to commit for the next 24 hours? Do you really want your Ideal Lifestyle? Remember, there is no in-between when it comes to success—time moves on. You are either working towards your Ideal Lifestyle, or you are moving away from it. If you're ready to commit, go ahead and sign your name.

Congratulations! Give yourself credit for what you've just done. You have clarity. You know what you want, and you know why you want it. You might not be clear yet on exactly how to get to the top of the mountain (that's what the other Maps are for) but at least you know what the ideal will feel like when you get there.

Most importantly, you are in control. You are committing to dream-based decisions and not fear-based ones. If you really want the ideal, you must feel it, you must virtualize it, and you must keep that feeling with you as much as possible.

Give yourself another big pat on the back. Maybe it took you a long time this first go-round, but it gets easier. I can do my Clarity Map in five concentrated minutes, everyday. Nothing feels as good as clarity.

TEACHING IS THE SHORTCUT TO LEARNING

If you want to further solidify this lesson, then I strongly encourage you to teach these principles to someone else. I can hear you grumbling. I know, I know, you sat down to read, not to teach. Well, get over it. Most people are hesitant to act, to do, to begin. They are frozen in

"If you can't explain it to a six year old, you don't understand it yourself."

— Albert Einstein —

place, afraid of failure and rejection. I don't want you to be "most people." Part of this "doing" book involves you getting out and sharing the Four Maps with other people. The sooner you teach something, the easier it becomes to do.

So find someone—anyone—in the next 24 hours and teach him or her how to draw a Clarity Map. It doesn't have to be perfect. In fact, it's better if it's very simple.

I won't keep repeating this teaching invitation for each of the Maps, but I did want to include it after the first one because teaching is the absolute fastest way to make the material your own.

Also, when you teach, you see the process from the eyes of a teacher. Often, this activates the "doer" in you. So, stop reading and go find someone to teach. And, if you can't find someone, then take out a blank piece of paper and teach it to yourself ☺.

STEP-BY-STEP RECAP

After each of the Four Maps I'll include a step-by-step shorthand recap to help you with the key aspects of the diagram. So, to draw your Clarity Map, here is what you need to do:

1. Draw your "before" and "after" frowny and smiley faces, and put the smiley face in the dream home, surrounded by the markers of an Ideal Lifestyle.

2. Write down three (3) of your "wants."

3. Write down three (3) of your "don't wants."

4. Write down three (3) of the personalized reasons why you are striving for your Ideal Lifestyle.

5. Virtualize, with all five senses, what your life will be like when you are living your Ideal Lifestyle.

6. Virtualize, with all five senses, yourself and the people you love benefitting from your hard work.

7. Make a 24-hour commitment to going after your Ideal Lifestyle, and sign your name.

MAP 2 ANTICIPATION

HOW TO DEVELOP AN INVINCIBLE ATTITUDE

WE AREN'T in control of what is going to be thrown at us in any given day, but we are absolutely in control of how we choose to respond to it. If we can get our brain to respond to challenges the way successful people respond to challenges, then we will eventually be successful. It's simple, but it's true.

The second map, the Anticipation Map, is about attitude. It's about approaching your day with the right mindset. It's about preparing your mind for the challenges you're going to confront today. But, you won't only face challenges today—you'll also come across wonderful opportunities. The Anticipation Map is going to help you become more receptive and grateful for those opportunities. When you've finished you'll have a game plan for overcoming any challenge that would try to stop you, and you'll feel confident that good things are coming for you. The Anticipation Map is your daily key to positivity, and to a realistic (yet still optimistic) approach to life.

CHALLENGES AND CHAMPIONS

Have you heard of the "Hero's Journey"? Maybe you aren't familiar with the work of Dr. Joseph Campbell (who popularized the concept), but if you've ever read a fairy tale or been told a bedtime story then you probably know all about the hero's journey. A brave soul sets out to accomplish something that seems impossible. Maybe they have to slay a dragon or stop a war between two kingdoms. Often the hero faces very long odds, and usually there are huge obstacles. Success is like that.

But a funny thing happens in every fairy tale, right when the hero is facing the longest odds, and right when defeat seems imminent: A champion appears to help the hero out. Sometimes the champion gives a piece of needed advice, points the way, or nurses the hero's wounds. We aren't alone on our journey to our Ideal Lifestyle. Yes, there are challenges, but at every step along our way, champions are waiting in the wings to help us. Sadly, sometimes we're so focused on our challenges, on the fire-breathing and fear-breathing dragons in front of us, that we completely ignore the

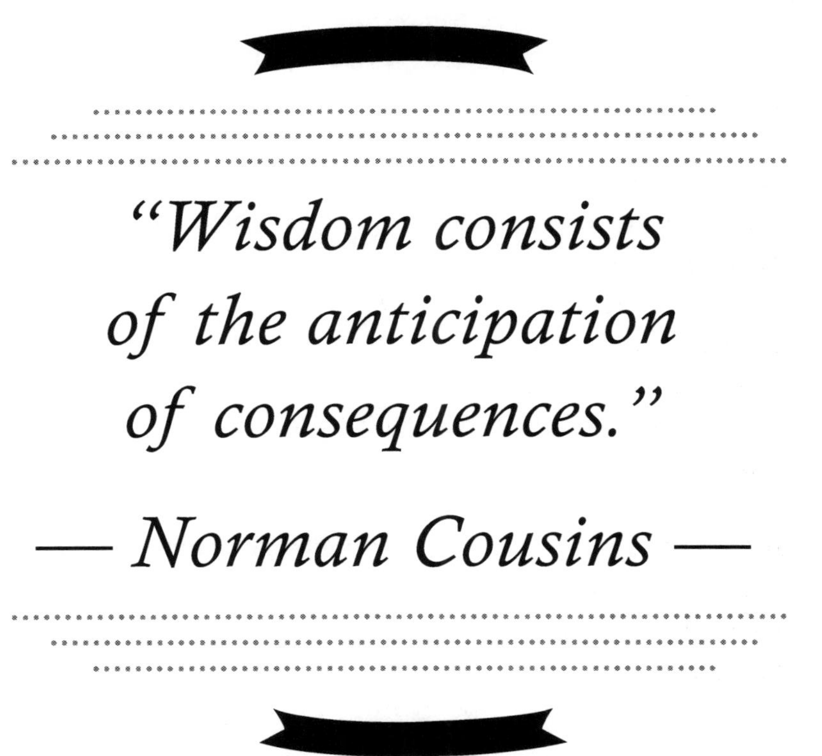
"Wisdom consists
of the anticipation
of consequences."
— Norman Cousins —

champions who are on our side. In the Anticipation Map, we're going to virtualize our champions as well as anticipate the challenges. I want you to become the kind of person who trusts that help is coming, even while you prepare for all obstacles. I want you to be savvy and hopeful at the same time. Not a pessimist, but a pragmatic optimist. That kind of person never fails to succeed.

So, let's draw your Anticipation Map. Once again, get out a blank piece of paper and a pen, or your favorite digital device. This first part is going to sound pretty familiar. In the top left hand portion write "Anticipation Map." Then, I want you to draw the exact same picture of the frowny face in the limiting box, and the smiley face in the dream home, surrounded by the symbols of an Ideal Lifestyle. Then I want you to draw the slope up the mountain, connecting the two. This is your hero's journey. Along the slope up the mountain, in the same place where you wrote, "Feel the Ideal" in your Clarity Map, I want you to write "Trust and Prepare." That's the theme of the Anticipation Map. We'll be touching on it as we go along. So far, your map should look something like this:

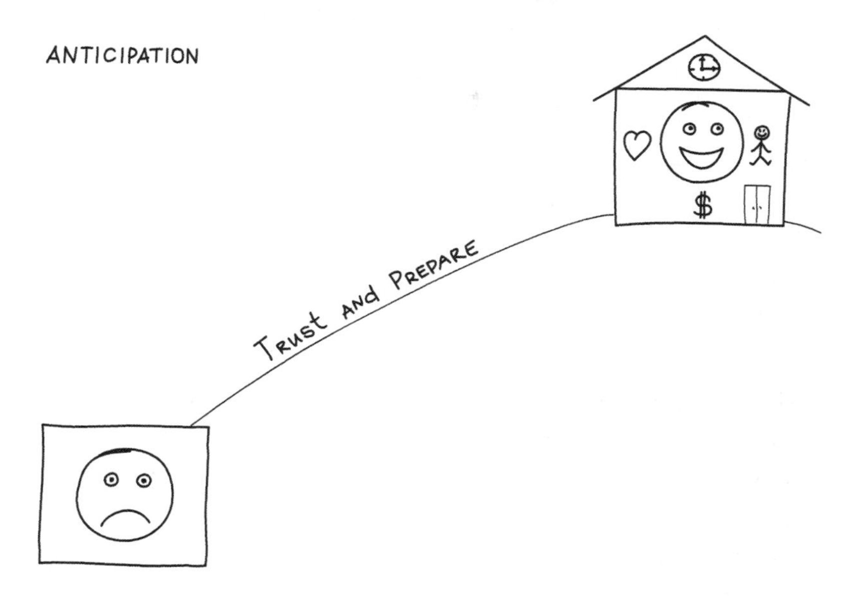

"NAMING" YOUR CHALLENGES

Wouldn't it be nice if our journey to the Ideal Lifestyle were a gentle stroll up the slope of the mountain? Maybe with a few stops for lemonade on the way? Sadly, that's not the case. It's often hard. It's full of obstacles on the way to the top. Your hero's journey is going to be harder than you hope and longer than you want. It's going to be costlier in time and money that you think you can afford, and higher than you thought you'd have to climb. I don't want to sugarcoat it.

But just because success is hard doesn't mean we can't prepare for the difficulty. Part of overcoming difficulty

"For which of you, intending to build a tower, sitteth not down first, and counteth the cost, whether he have sufficient to finish it?."

— Luke 14:28-30 —

is having powerful reasons behind your actions, which is why we spent so much time defining our reasons in the Clarity Map. Very few obstacles can slow you down when you have powerful reason engines.

Another big part of success is preparing for your challenges—specifically "naming" your challenges. A magical thing happens to challenges when you name and anticipate them: They lose their discouraging power. They don't surprise you and leave you suddenly crestfallen. They become just one more thing you had planned for, one more little annoyance on your path towards your Ideal Lifestyle. When you were a kid were you worried about the boogeyman in the closet? Were you afraid of the dark? If so, what happened when you turned on the light? Not much of a problem then, was it? There are certain types of challenges that we all face, so why not prepare for them?

There is powerful neuroscience, as well as centuries of spiritual and religious tradition, behind this concept of pre-planning for obstacles. It's also often called the management of expectations. Nothing can surprise and discourage us if we prepare for anything and everything.

At the end of the Anticipation Map you're going to name your day's specific challenges. But, before we get there, I want to share with you the types of challenges you might face. I want you to draw them on your

Anticipation Map, to prepare you to face them. I find that most challenges in life fall into five categories:

THE FIVE MAJOR CHALLENGES

Challenge 1: The Whirlwind

If you're like me, you're up and running from the moment the sun comes up until long after it has set. Too much to do and too little time to do it. That's life. It's in your face, 24/7. It's hard to break out of the box of our "before" self because we're engulfed in a whirlwind of daily distractions and responsibilities.

My mentor, Stephen Covey, called it the Urgent vs. the Important. The urgent little deadlines—like laundry and email—that pop up every day, screaming at you, distracting you from the things that are really important. It's a wonder that anyone accomplishes anything important in the middle of this daily whirlwind, but a few do.

If you want to do something important—something off in the distance—you have to squeeze out some time for it today—in the middle of the whirlwind. You have to choose your ideal in the face of so many daily demands. It takes focus, determination, stamina, and sacrifice.

If you want an abundant harvest tomorrow, you've got to plant some seeds today—no matter how many urgent things are on your to-do list. Like a hero, you tirelessly fight back the whirlwind to carve out a few essential moments.

On your Anticipation Map, I want you to draw the whirlwind. Go back to your frowny face and draw some swirly lines obscuring the face, like Pig-Pen in the old Peanuts comics. It might look like this:

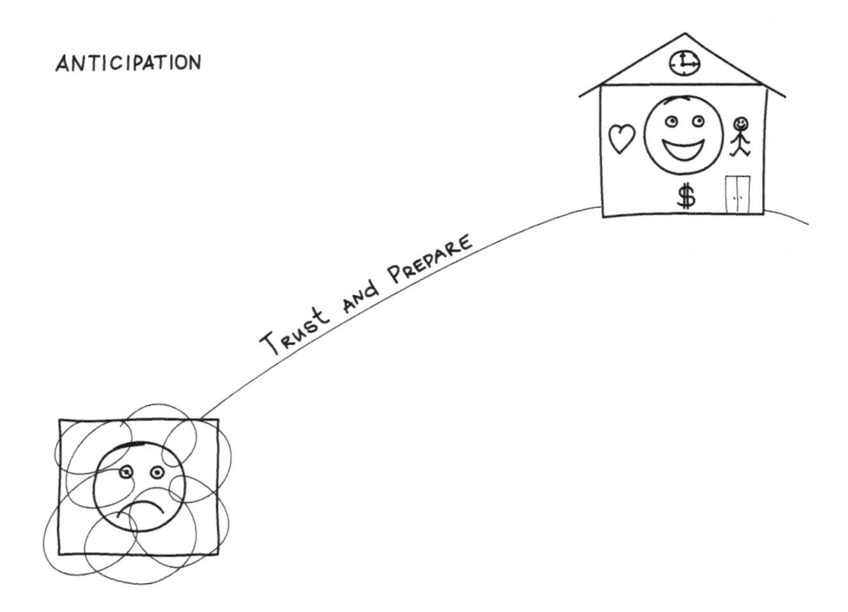

Everyday you are going to have to deal with a whirlwind of urgent things that, in the long run, aren't the important things that are going to help you reach your Ideal

Lifestyle. Now you know the challenge, now you've "named" the challenge, and now you can prepare.

Challenge #2 The Learning Curve

We're going to illustrate the next few obstacles via a different trail up the mountain. There is no straight shot up to your Ideal Lifestyle. Often there are switchbacks. The line I want you to draw is a bit difficult to describe, so I'm just going to show it to you—it's our route up the mountain. Each curve on this line represents a different challenge, which we'll soon dive into. For now, draw a long dip up the middle of your mountain, followed by a couple of switchbacks. It's going to look like this:

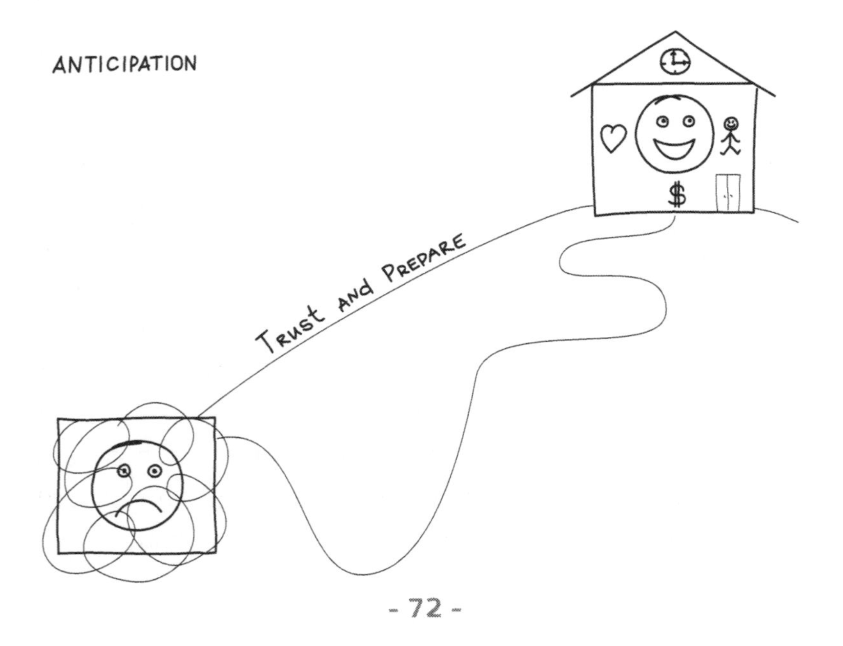

Let's say you find a way to escape the whirlwind. You do the important things first. You break out of your box and start your climb. What's the next challenge? It comes up almost immediately:

When you choose to improve your life, you almost always attempt to learn some new skill. For instance, suppose you launch a new business in a new industry. There is going to be a period of time when you are taking your lumps. As with any new skill, there is a learning curve.

On your Anticipation Map, that first line that dips—that is the learning curve. You're going to look foolish for a while. You'll fail a lot while you practice the way to mastery. A learning curve can last weeks, months or years. Can you make it through this zone? You can, if you anticipate it.

If you quit during a learning curve, it often puts you worse off than before you began. Some people get caught in a painful cycle of committing to a new life, beginning the difficult path, but then stopping because the learning curve is too steep. If you give up partway through, then your self-esteem is going to take a major hit. You'll probably feel like a failure. You might think you are "snake-bit" or cursed. You aren't. No one is inherently a failure. That's fear talking. You just need to keep fighting through the learning curve.

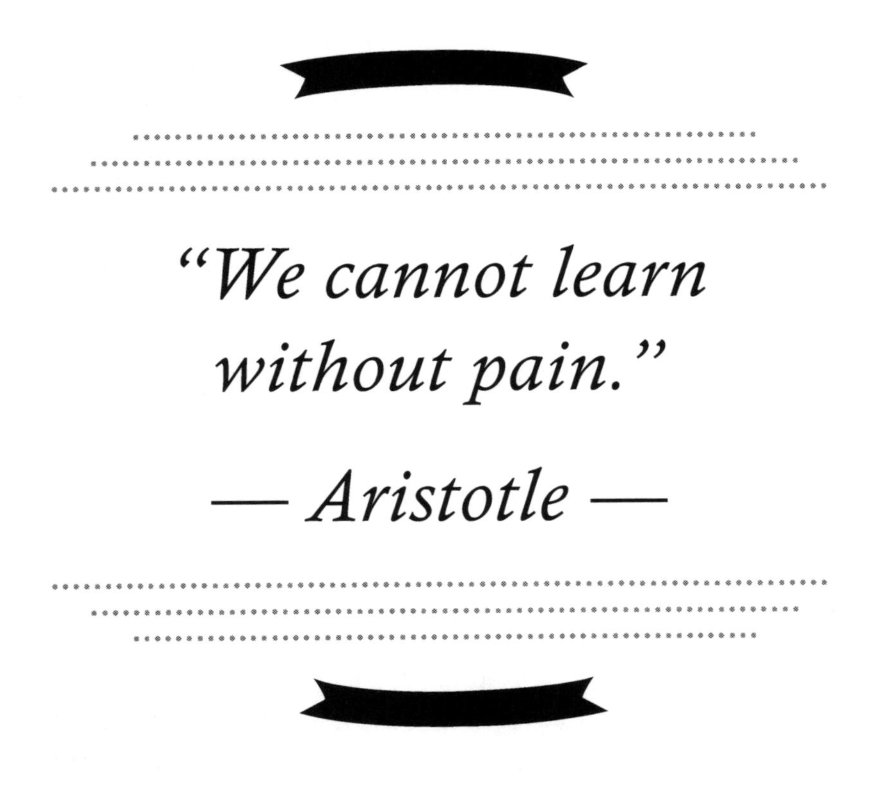
"We cannot learn
without pain."
— Aristotle —

To illustrate the learning curve and what happens if you quit, I want you to draw another frowny face to the right of the steepest part of the curve. This represents somebody who stops, who gets spit out, who doesn't push through. It should look like this:

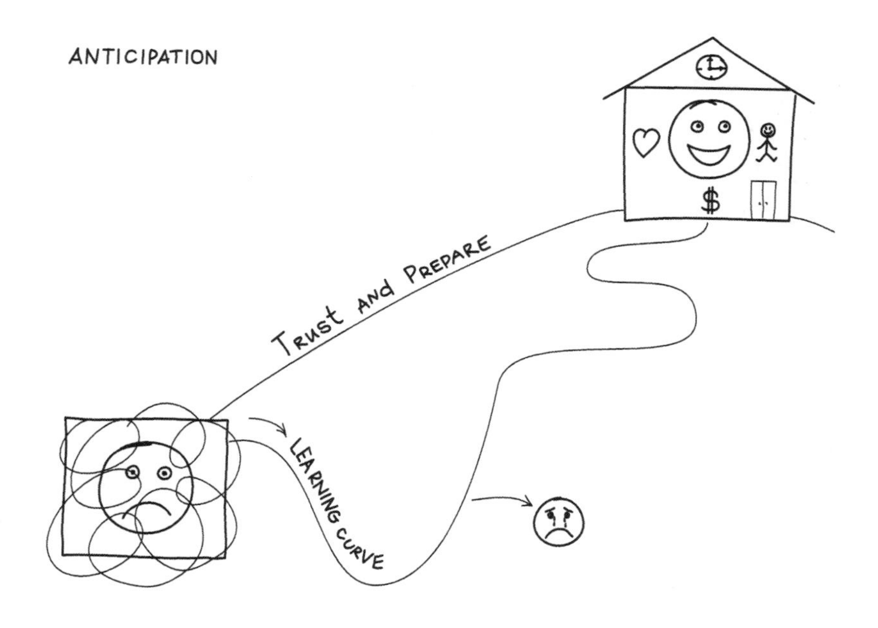

Here's a secret about learning a new skill: Acquiring the skill is not the main goal. Actually, the objective is becoming, right now, the kind of person who is determined to acquire the skill, and then never forgetting that you have committed to become that person. The skill will naturally follow your commitment.

The best thing about learning curves is that they eventually end ☺. Once through the learning curve, there is rapid ascent. You are on your way to the top.

Challenge #3 The Marshmallows

A few decades ago, Walter Mischel of Stanford University conducted a series of famous experiments with 500 young children, aged 4-6. Researchers placed these young children alone in a room with a marshmallow on the table in front of them. They could eat the marshmallow right then, or, if they could just wait a few minutes (delay their gratification) until the researcher returned, they could have two marshmallows. Could they wait?

Two-thirds of them could not—when the researcher returned the marshmallow had been devoured. What about the one-third who resisted? You've probably seen the hilarious YouTube™ videos of children struggling to avoid eating the marshmallows. Turns out that the one-third who succeeded had advanced strategies for distracting themselves. But the story doesn't stop there.

The researchers followed these youngsters for decades and monitored their progress every ten years. Those who had the willpower to resist the marshmallow also had the willpower in other areas of their lives. They had better relationships, better health, were more organized with their time, had better grades, and earned substantially more money in their careers.

What? All this because they refused a marshmallow?

It's true that good things come to those who wait. It's also true that *better* things come to those who wait. Do you have the will to delay your reward until it doubles or triples or quadruples? That's the essence of wealth—delaying gratification and investing for the future.

The world has gotten magnitudes more persuasive than a mere marshmallow. There are virtual marshmallows everywhere. To have willpower in these modern times takes much more courage. This is the age of distraction. It nibbles away at your resolve every second of every day. Do you have the willpower?

The next Map, the Ritual Map, is going to focus on building world-class willpower. For now, I just want you to recognize that there are going to be marshmallows on your hero's journey. And you're going to have to say "no" now so you can get more sweetness later.

Back on your drawing, I want you to draw a single marshmallow in the middle of the path, right after the learning curve. It's there to remind you, so you can prepare for today's metaphorical marshmallows. Notice that the path goes around it, and you can too.

Here is what your Anticipation Map might look like with the marshmallow:

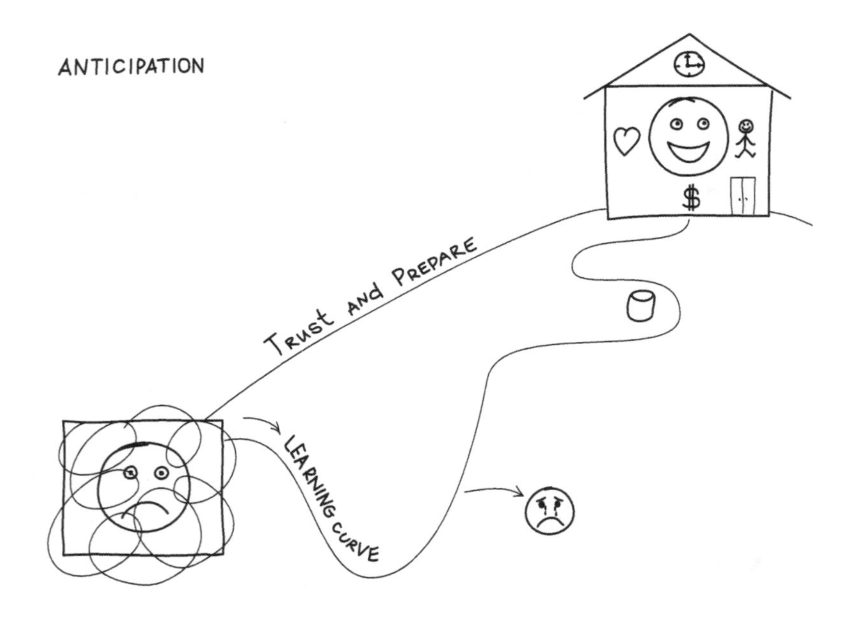

Challenge #4 The Cliff

When I was a young boy, my father used to take me fishing in Waterton Lakes National Park in Alberta, Canada. One weekend we decided to hike to Lineham Lakes, a famous set of three lakes set in a basin above a 300-foot cliff. Few fishermen dared cross the cliff, but those who did experienced the best fishing of their lives. The fish were large and hungry, and most of them had never seen a hook ☺. I braved the cliffs just once. It was terrifying. But I'll never forget that day. The fishing was exhilarating.

That's the way it is with opportunity. The best opportunities are always hidden behind terrifying cliffs. In the real world, cliffs can be things that inspire fear—like public speaking, or quitting your job, or opening your own practice—and cliffs can also be things that seem incredibly inconvenient, like learning a new language or relocating to a city with better opportunities.

Opportunity often knocks when we think we are least ready, inside and out. It shows up when we can't afford it, when we're too busy, when we don't feel well, when the people around us are opposed to it, when it's inconvenient. Why do the best opportunities seem hidden behind the cliffs of inconvenience?

The cliffs exist to discourage the "fair weather" fishers. Where anyone can fish, the fish are smaller and less plentiful. Beyond the cliffs, the fish are bigger, because no one dares fish there—except the few. Are you in the final group? Do you want to be? Decide to be.

Go ahead and draw three or four vertical lines right on top of the last switchback on your Anticipation Map. These are the cliffs—they are there to remind you that every goal worth achieving will force you at some point to face what terrifies you. Most people will turn back, but you won't—if you have clarity, and if you anticipate what's coming. Here is how your Anticipation Map might look:

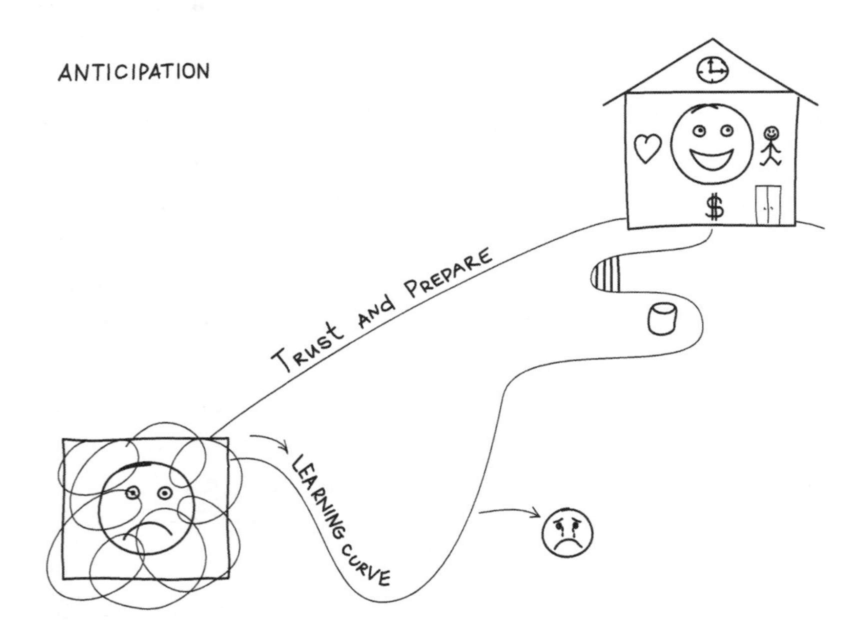

Challenge #5 The Sudden Storm

Let's suppose you master a new skill and you're on your way. Momentum is building. You've avoided the marshmallows and you've even climbed up the cliff of what terrifies you. You're right there near the summit, almost to the goal of your hero's journey. Then, something terrible happens. You get sick. There's been an accident. Or, maybe you just have a bad day.

Followed by a bad week or a bad month. Your vision blurs. *A better life? What was I thinking?!*

We all get blindsided by things we could never anticipate. Something horrible happens to us or to the people we love. That's the sudden storm. But, while we can't anticipate exactly what the sudden storm will be, we *can* anticipate that there will *be* a sudden storm. See what we did there? It's a neat little trick of the mind that makes a huge difference. We can prepare for the unknown even if it remains unknown. Even the completely unknown can be stripped of its power to surprise and discourage. "Oh hi, sudden storm," we can say when disaster strikes, "you look nasty, but hey, I knew you were coming, so I brought my umbrella."

Sudden storms are going to happen in each and every life. Sometimes they knock us off the path momentarily. But, if we draw our Clarity and Anticipation Maps every day, we can quickly get back on track.

However, if we've lost our clarity, we are in danger of letting the sudden storms blow us off of the slopes for weeks, months, or even years. We lose our vision and we bump along through life. Everybody knows what this is like. Every day we meet people (sometimes in the mirror) who had a vision for their life, were on their hero's journey, faced a sudden storm, lost their clarity, and paused their quest. Now they wander through life,

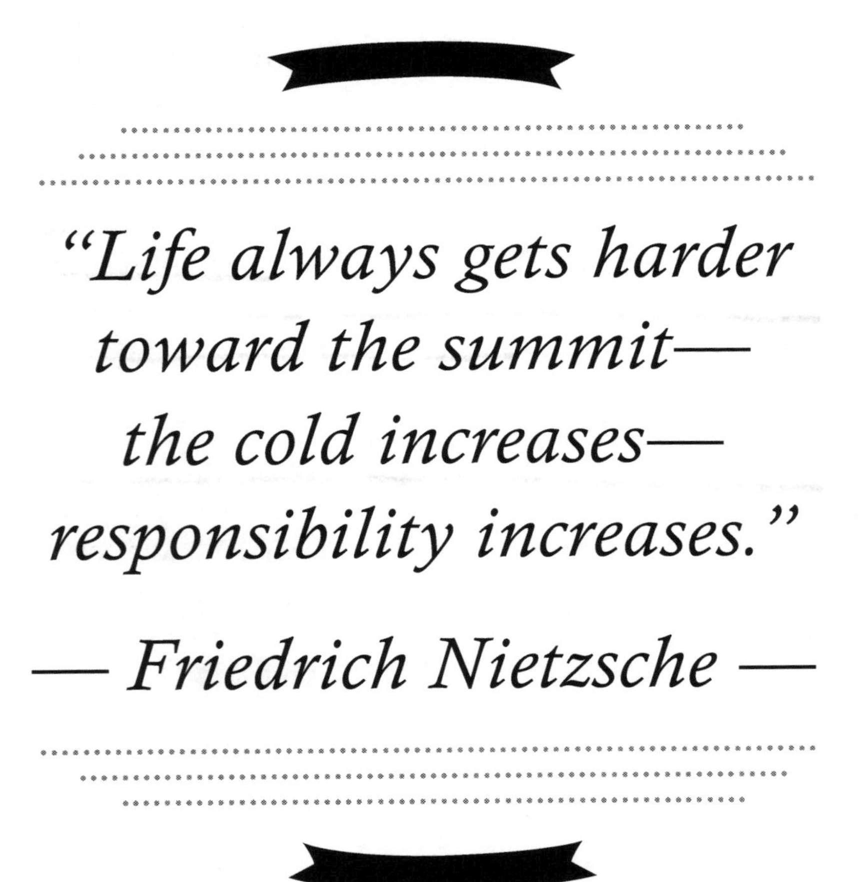
"Life always gets harder
toward the summit—
the cold increases—
responsibility increases."
— Friedrich Nietzsche —

without purpose or direction. Millions, even billions, of dreams have been waylaid by sudden storms.

Hopefully you are drawing the Four Maps, to keep reminding you of where you want to be, and why you need to get there. Clarity is the antidote for even the worst sudden storm.

To illustrate the sudden storm on your Anticipation Map, I want you to draw a cloud just to the left of the learning curve, with a lightning bolt shooting out, trying to knock you off the path. It might look something like this:

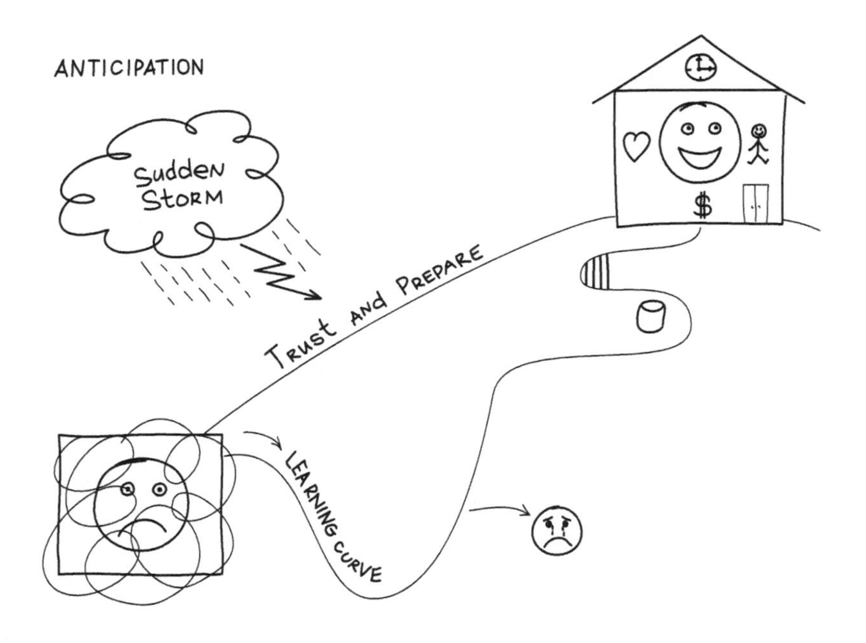

WRITE DOWN YOUR CHALLENGES

Hopefully you've been thinking of some of your day's specific obstacles as we've been going over the five major types of challenges.

On your Anticipation Map, to the right of the marshmallow, I want you to write "Challenges" followed by three (3) blank lines below it. It might look like this:

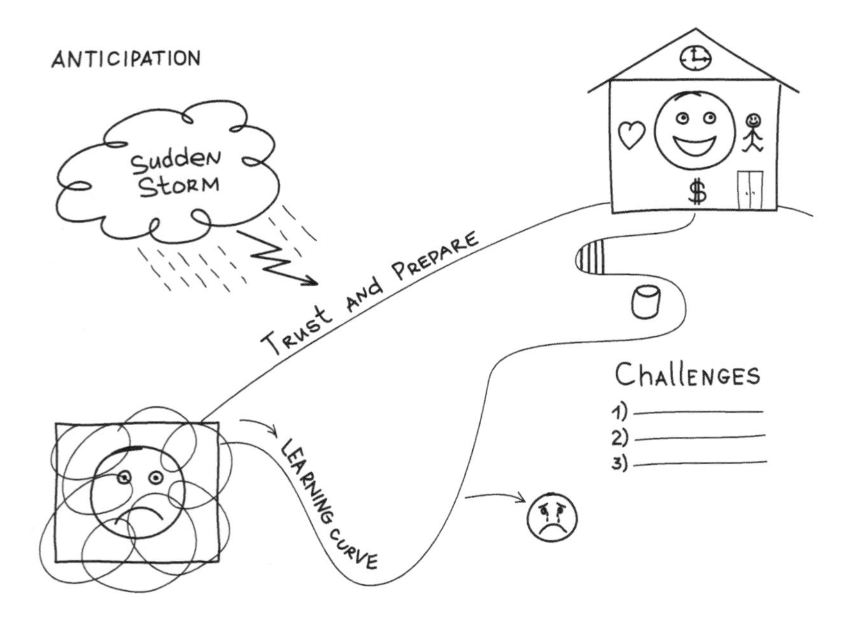

Write down three (3) of your day's challenges and, as you write them, commit inside yourself that you will overcome them. For example, if you are trying to lose weight, one of your challenges might be the cookies that a neighbor brought over. If you are trying to learn a new skill, one of your challenges today might be the whirlwind of your favorite time-wasting website. Every day your challenges are going to change slightly.

I don't want you to virtualize these challenges as you write them because I don't want you to think them into reality. Let's not play with fire. But I do want you to virtualize your reaction to the challenges. What happens when you face a challenge that you already know is coming, a challenge that you have "named"? It rolls right off your back. It doesn't have the power to discourage you because you've prepared for it and already decided that it isn't strong enough to stop you. You step into the imaginary shoes of all the heroes before who have climbed difficult slopes. This journey you've chosen is not for the weak or timid. This is the hero's journey. This takes courage.

But you're not alone on this journey. My favorite part of the Anticipation Map is virtualizing your champions.

YOU HAVE CHAMPIONS

Even if we have trouble believing it, everyone on earth has champions waiting in the wings to help. Everyone has good things coming. Even the loneliest of us has

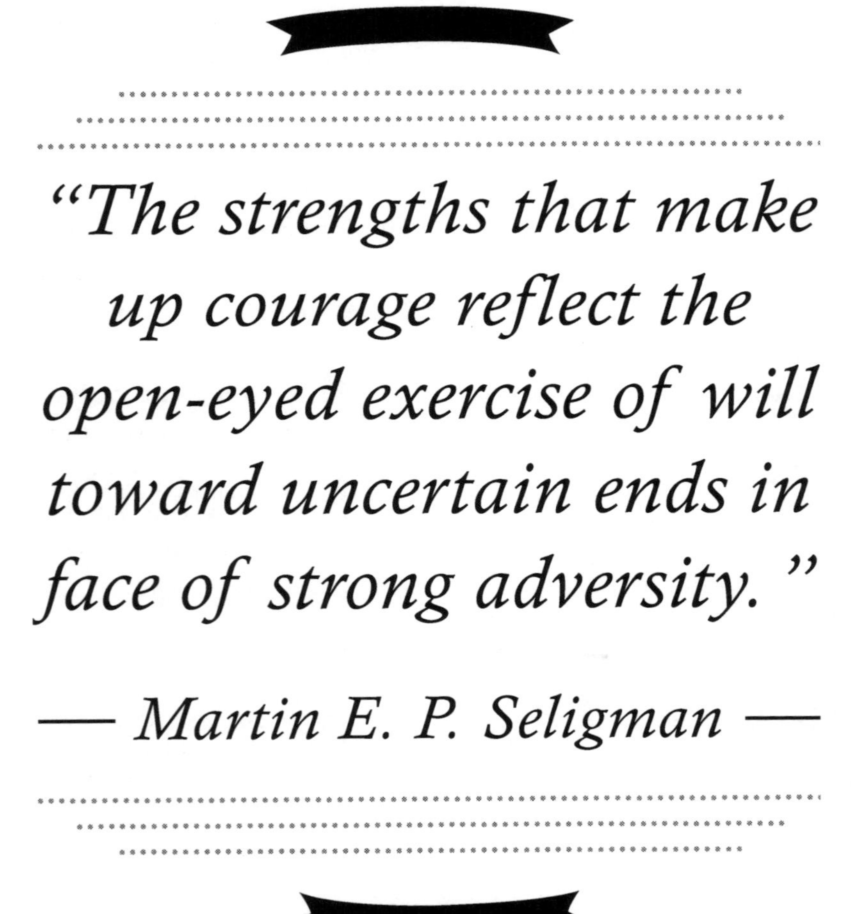
"The strengths that make up courage reflect the open-eyed exercise of will toward uncertain ends in face of strong adversity."
— Martin E. P. Seligman —

champions, because our champions aren't necessarily people. Sometimes a champion is an opportunity, or a sunset, or a good book, or a lucky break, a guardian angel, or the sale that comes just in time. Are you the sort of person who believes in abundance—who believes that good things are coming?

On your Anticipation Map, I want you to write "Champions" in the space to the right of your sudden storm, with three (3) blank lines below it. It might look like this:

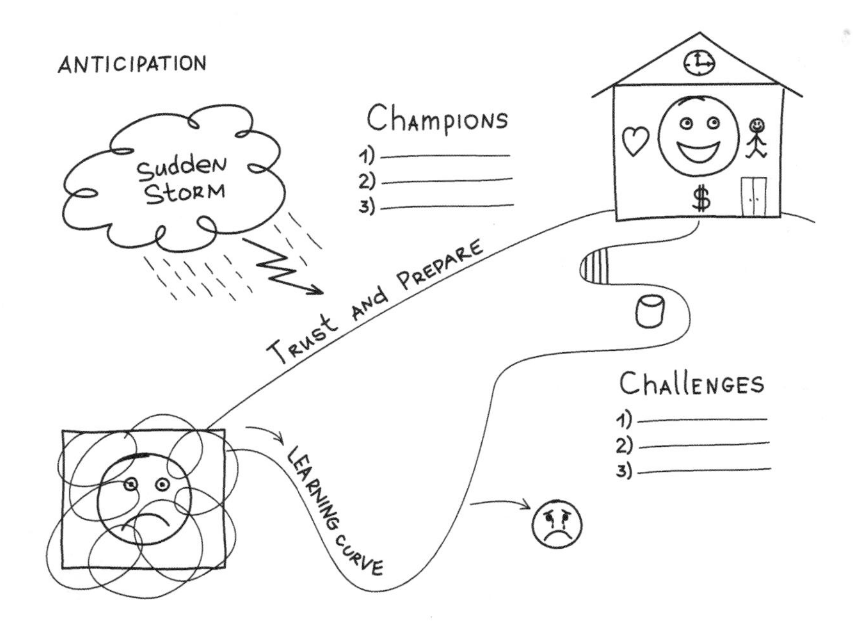

Next comes a very important part of your Anticipation Map. It's time for another feel-the-ideal personal meditation. I want you to think deeply about who and what your champions are today. Do you have people who are pulling for you? Are there good things that might happen to you today? Do you have an inkling of what they are? Right now, I want you to think about your champions, and I want you to virtualize them as if they had already stepped in to help you. Close your eyes, just like we did in the Clarity Map. Really concentrate. As you virtualize the good things coming your way, write them down in the blank lines.

Then take it one more step: Pause for a second and try to feel deep gratitude for the champions you've written down, whether they are people or events or gifts.

The only thing left to do on our Anticipation Map is to sign it, and to make the commitment. But, before we do that, I want to talk a little more about the power of gratitude. Giving thanks for your champions, real and imagined, is probably the most important step of the Anticipation Map. Here's why:

THE POWER OF GRATITUDE

My experience has shown me that deep, daily gratitude creates powerful, instant transformation in the quality of my life. But I don't have to rely only on my experience. The latest neuroscience, as well as thousands of years of religious and spiritual tradition, is firmly behind the miracle of gratitude.

Even the slightest bit of gratitude in the moment makes it impossible to run a fear-based mindset. Gratitude is the antidote to fear. When we don't have gratitude we are prone to woe-is-me thinking. We can feel victimized by others, or by chance and circumstance. I don't know any successful people who run a fear-based mindset, so it stands to reason that I don't know any successful people who see themselves as victims in any way. Yes, life gives you lemons sometimes, and, contrary to the old saying, the secret isn't to make them into lemonade. The secret is to *love lemons.* Successful people are always grateful.

I had to learn the lesson of gratitude the very hard way. In March of 2003, I was driving home through a rainstorm to my house in San Diego. I was on the freeway in the fast lane. It was, as the novels say, a dark and stormy night. I lost control of my luxury coupe and flew off the road. I went down a steep embankment and slammed head-on into the thick trunk of a mesquite tree. The impact caved in the front of my car and put the engine in my lap. I shattered my wrist, severed my quadriceps, cracked my spine and was scalped by the rear-view mirror. They had to use the jaws of life to get me out of the car, and the only reason they knew I was there is because one Good Samaritan had seen my car go down the slope and had turned around to come find me and call the police. My car, when it stopped, wasn't visible from the road.

My accident was certainly quite the sudden storm. For the first few years after my accident I felt enormous gratitude, as you can imagine, for the people (true champions) who saved my life—the good Samaritan, the doctors, blood donors, nurses, and my family. That gratitude helped me push through some dark days of physical rehabilitation. Every day I found myself whispering under my breath, *thank you, thank you, thank you, thank you*—hundreds of times a day. I felt so grateful for every breath. Years later, I still find myself tearing up and saying silent *thank-yous*.

But a funny thing happened after those first few years. I maintained my gratitude for my physical saviors, but I also started to feel deep gratitude for the accident itself. I know that might sound crazy, but my wreck changed me as a person—for the better. I began to care even more about the things that really mattered. I began to be less finance-focused, and more determined to help anyone and everyone I could reach. I believe my accident happened for a reason, and without it I could never have written this book.

Gratitude is so powerful that it has the ability to transform our challenges from things we fear to things we look forward to! We can actually look forward to horrible things if we have a gratitude mindset, because we know that, in the long run, challenges will actually help us. "What doesn't kill me only makes me stronger" is a time-tested aphorism because it's true. What's also true is that what doesn't kill you can often make you more grateful.

I urge you to take the time in your Anticipation Map to let gratitude, even for your challenges, flood into your heart. This is next-level thinking, but if you are committed to gratitude then you can come to love even your challenges. And what happens when you love a challenge? It's no longer a challenge—it's a champion. You can look forward to it, knowing in the long run that it will work out in your favor. Master the art of gratitude and you can erase every challenge and have a life (and hero's journey) full of nothing but champions. That's true transformation.

MAKE THE COMMITMENT

Okay, let's recap. You realize you're on a hero's journey, full of challenges and wonderful, timely champions. You've become familiar with the five major types of challenges and you've drawn them so you'll remember them. You've thought deeply about your day and anticipated certain challenges you might face, like maybe a whirlwind urgent event (a TV show, or a sporting event) threatens to pull you away from what's important. You've written down your challenges and determined to overcome them. You've also taken some time to meditate and prepare your mind to receive today's champions. You've written down three things today that are ready to help you, and you've hopefully paused in a moment of deep gratitude for all you've been given—the champions and the challenges.

Take a breath. How do you feel? Do you feel ready to face your day? Do you feel prepared for your hero's journey? Remember, you are heading to your Ideal Lifestyle—your own best self. Make the 24-hour commitment to doing your best today by signing your Anticipation Map. It should look like this:

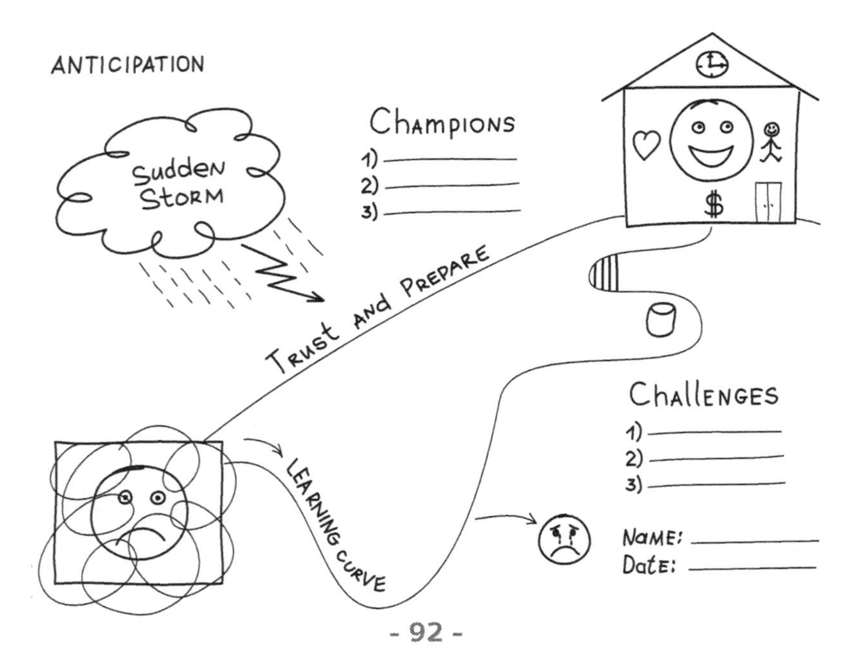

Congratulations. I'm proud of you. You have clarity—you know where you are going—and you know what's coming to help and hinder you. You have the attitude of the most successful people on earth. You're ready to act. Do you feel ready to act? You'd better, because the last two Maps are all about making it happen ☺.

STEP-BY-STEP RECAP

In review, to draw your Anticipation Map, here is what you need to do:

1. Draw your "before" and "after" frowny and smiley faces, and put the smiley face in the dream home, surrounded by the markers of an Ideal Lifestyle.
2. Draw a different path up the mountain and fill that path with the five major types of challenges.
3. Write down three (3) of today's possible challenges.
4. Virtualize, with all five senses, overcoming these challenges.
5. Write down three (3) of today's possible champions.
6. Virtualize, with all five senses, these champions coming to help you in your day's moment of need.
7. Take a moment to feel deep gratitude for your life, for your champions, and even for your challenges.
8. Make a 24-hour commitment to living with anticipation, overcoming obstacles, and embracing champions. Sign your name to demonstrate your commitment.

MAP 3 RITUAL

HOW TO GET THE ESSENTIAL THINGS DONE EVERYDAY

UP UNTIL NOW we've been talking about your mindset, about your attitudes, and about your motivation. The Clarity Map is about getting your mind focused on your Ideal Lifestyle, and the Anticipation Map is about preparing your mind to be receptive to good things, and to be impervious to disappointment from any possible challenges. That's about where most self-improvement books stop. But not this one. I'm determined to teach you everything you need to get to the top of the mountain of your life.

And what you need, now that your mind is right, is to take *action*. You need to get things done in the real world, outside of your mind. The final two maps are all about getting things done—taking action.

HABIT AND TASK

All the actions of our lives break down into two key categories: Repeated daily actions—our habits—and specific, project-oriented tasks. Everything we do is either a habit or a task. Yup, every single step we take falls into one of these two categories.

Here's how it works in a tiny example: Let's say you want perfect, white teeth. A beautiful set of chompers is on your bucket list ☺. Well, you would obviously need a set of habits, things you do everyday, to maintain your teeth. You would brush and floss and use a good mouthwash. But that's not enough, even if you do it everyday, to have perfect teeth. At some point, you are going to get a cavity and need to fix it. Going to the dentist to fill that cavity is a task—a targeted, "one-time" action. You don't quit your routine and stop brushing your teeth just because you have a cavity—no way, you keep at it—but you couldn't achieve your perfect smile with only routine. You can't have perfect teeth until you combine good habits with specific tasks.

Success is the same way. Our habits are the base of all success, and then specific, project-based tasks take us on our personalized path up the mountain to our Ideal Lifestyle.

The Ritual Map is all about building a powerful, personalized set of success habits. When we get through with the next drawing, you'll have developed a daily ritual, as well as a deep understanding of the value of consistent, repeated action.

Habit and ritual are having a bit of a moment in neuroscience, as more and more studies are released that point to the correlation between ritual and success. In my own life, I have seen this play out time and time again. I want to dive in and teach you why ritual is so powerful, as it relates to personal growth and business.

SUCCESS IS COMPOUND INTEREST

The Ritual Map starts the same way that the first two maps started. Take a piece of blank paper (or device) and draw the now-familiar frowny face in the lower left hand corner and the smiley face in the top right. Put them in their respective limiting box and dream home. Look familiar? Go ahead and draw the mountain slope between the frowning face and the smiling face, just like you did in the other Maps. Along that line, I want you to write the phrase "Groove to Grow." That's our theme for the Ritual Map. It should look like this:

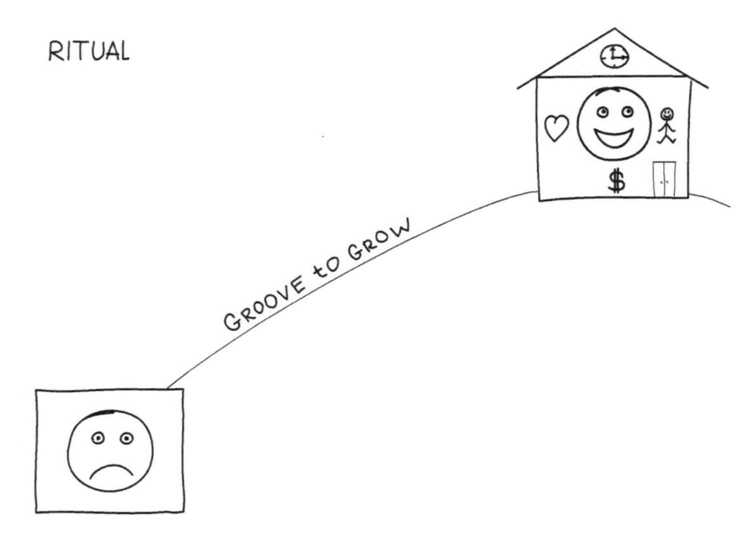

Now, I'm going to have you draw a path up the face of the mountain. The path is going to be a single long curve—an exponential curve. It starts out gradual and then shoots up to the summit of the mountain. It should look like this:

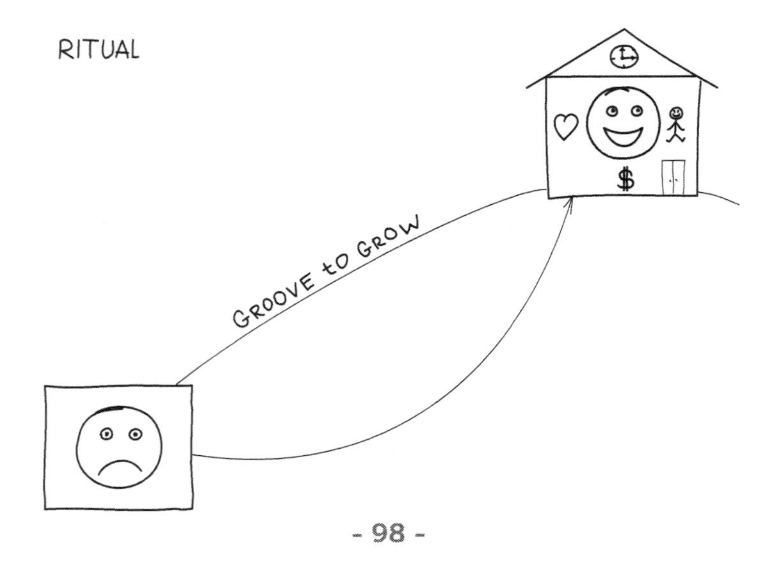

It's the curve of compound interest. It's there to remind you that a few things done consistently over time produce amazing results. I'm going to dip into my past and use some finance language to illustrate the principle. No doubt, you are aware of the power of compounding growth. But do you know the secret of how it works?

Suppose your parents had established a savings program for you on the day you were born that continued until your 66th birthday. Just depositing $1 a day in an ordinary bank account at 0% interest would accumulate a nest egg of about $25,000 in a lifetime. Look at what the same daily $1 grows into at various interest rates:

0%: $25,000
3%: $75,000
5%: $200,000
10%: $2,750,000
15%: $50,000,000
20%: $1,000,000,000

Did you get that? Just a measly $1 a day invested at 20% grows into one BILLION dollars in a lifetime.

But having a high interest rate is not the secret to compound growth. Look at the formula.

Regular deposits (X) Interest Rate = Exponential results

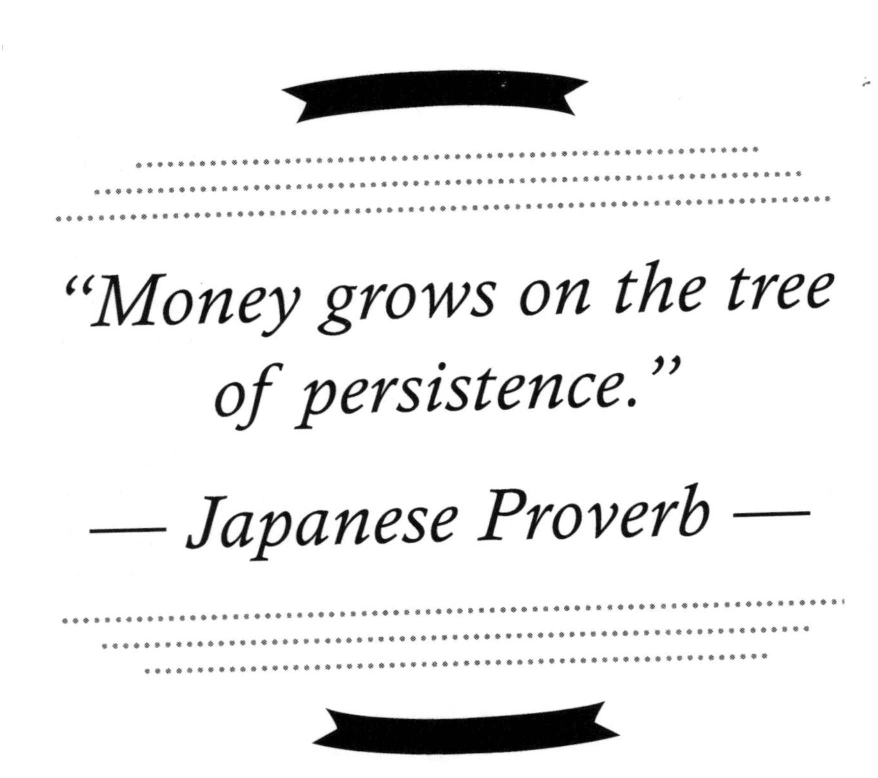

"Money grows on the tree of persistence."

— Japanese Proverb —

The secret to compound growth is the word "regular." If you stop the regular deposits, the power fizzles fast. 20% of zero is...zero.

Consistency is the magic word. Consistent Daily Deposits. One step in front of the other, day after day after day.

You'll see that the early growth along the curve is long and slow—almost imperceptible. But eventually growth starts to be visible—and increasing. The interest you earn (your growth) starts to earn interest. Your "money" is earning money for you. This continues until the growth curve turns upward in an almost vertical line of exponential growth.

I'm talking in business terms, but I'm also talking about your journey to your Ideal Lifestyle. Your habits, your ritual, is the way to invest in yourself. In business and life, consistency is the key to growth. Great business growth. Great sports achievement. Great musical performance. Great mastery of any skill.

THE ANT AND THE GRASSHOPPER

Every day as you draw your Ritual Map, I want you to be reminded of the power of consistent, daily habit. Go back to your Ritual Map and draw a little ant at the beginning of the exponential curve. It might look like this:

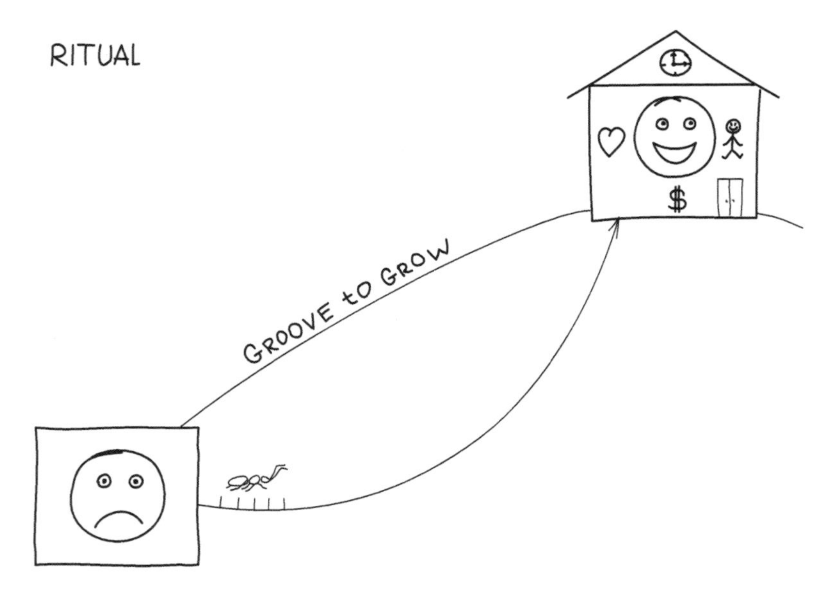

The ant is there to illustrate one of my favorite stories from Aesop's fables, The Ant and the Grasshopper. Perhaps you remember it?

"There was a smart little ant that worked every day to put food away for the winter. In the same forest, there was also a grasshopper. But, the grasshopper was a spendthrift that invested his time playing, taking no thought for the future. When winter arrived, the grasshopper starved and the ant thrived."

It's such a simple story, yet it teaches a lesson about the power of small things done consistently. Small, repeated action is the driving force behind prosperity. Every day you need to be determined enough to set

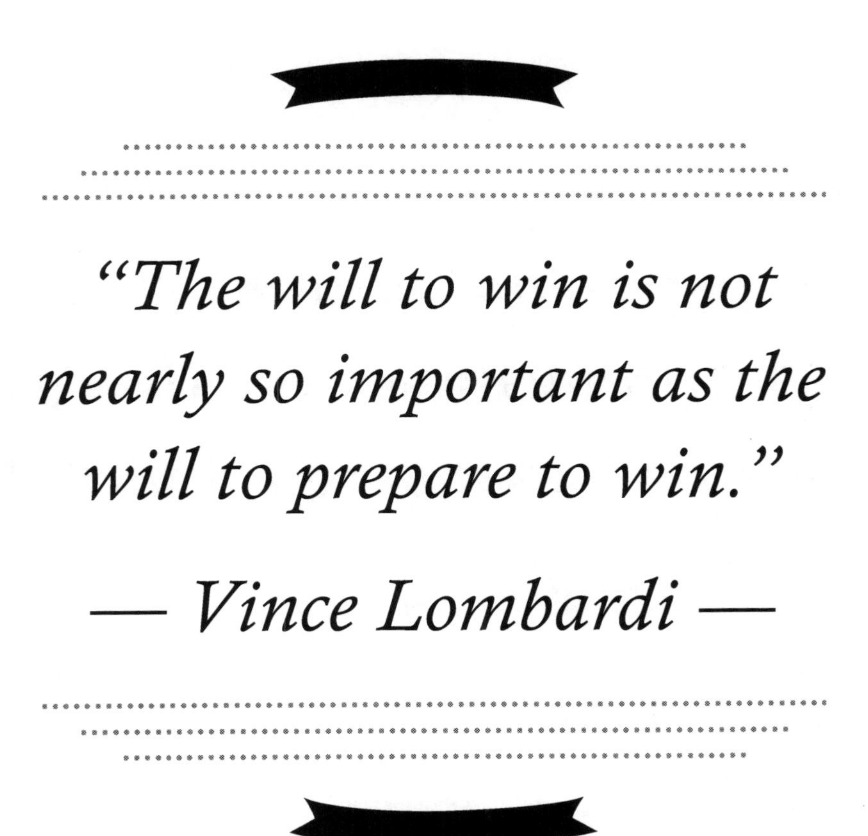
"The will to win is not nearly so important as the will to prepare to win."
— Vince Lombardi —

"My success is due more to my ability to work continuously on one thing without stopping than to any other single quality."

— Thomas Edison —

aside some "ant" time for your ritual. Time to get clear on your goals, anticipate your challenges, and work towards your Ideal Lifestyle.

So, if you haven't done so already, go draw the little ant at the very beginning of the compound interest curve, to remind you that it is the tiny, daily investments that grow into huge eventual rewards. You're not just preparing for winter—you're building a future of perpetual summer.

So, how do you carve a little "ant" time out of an already too-busy day? Where does the smart little ant find the will to act like an ant? The answer is simple. The ant has learned to prioritize.

BIG ROCKS

The most profound analogy I've ever learned on the subject of priorities is the Big Rocks Analogy made popular by Dr. Stephen Covey.

I was Professor Covey's research assistant when I was an undergraduate at Brigham Young University in 1972. He was a wonderful man who had a huge impact on my life. I remember sitting in his class and listening to him teach many of the concepts that would eventually find their way into his blockbuster bestseller, The Seven Habits of Highly Effective People. He challenged me to write down my goals in life. As one of my lifetime goals I wrote, "I will write a book." I knew it was something I wanted, even though, as a fresh-faced 23 year old, I couldn't see how I could possibly get there. Stephen Covey helped me get my internal life in order—he was an excellent teacher. I did manage to write a book, and I even had the enormous satisfaction of helping Stephen, years later, with some of the marketing strategy behind the release of Seven Habits.

You've probably read at least one variation of the Big Rocks Analogy—versions of it have been floating around a long time, maybe even as far back as the middle ages. But I prefer Stephen's take from his book, First Things First, which I highly recommend.

The story starts out with a professor in front of a group of students. She calls for a pop quiz, pulls out a one gallon, wide-mouthed mason jar, and sets it on the table. She takes three large rocks and places them carefully in the jar.

By this point the jar looks full, in the sense that no more big rocks are going to fit. The professor asks the class if the jar is full. They all say yes. With a twinkle in her eye the professor takes out a bag of gravel, dumps it into the jar, and shakes it around. The gravel fills all the spaces between the big rocks. "Is the jar full now?" the professor asks. The class says, "no." They are starting to catch on that the jar can hold even more.

The professor pulls out a cup of water and pours it into the rocks and gravel, filling the jar up to the brim. Now the jar is full and the professor tell the class that the jar represents an average day in life. Then she asks the class what they think the story means—what is the point of the story?

A student raises his hand and says something like, "No matter how full or busy your day is, you can always squeeze in a bit more stuff."

"No," the professor says. "The point actually far simpler. If you don't put the big rocks in first, before you put in the gravel and water, you'll never be able to fit them in."

What are the Big Rocks in your life? Do you put them in first? Or do you get distracted with little, urgent "whirlwind" things until you don't have the energy to tackle the important things?

I want you to go back to your Ritual Map. Take out your pen, and, in the bottom right corner of the page, draw an empty, wide-mouth jar. It doesn't have to look perfect. Just draw your best empty jar.

Now, fill the jar with several large circles—these are the big rocks. Underneath the jar, I want you to write "Big Rocks First." It should look something like this:

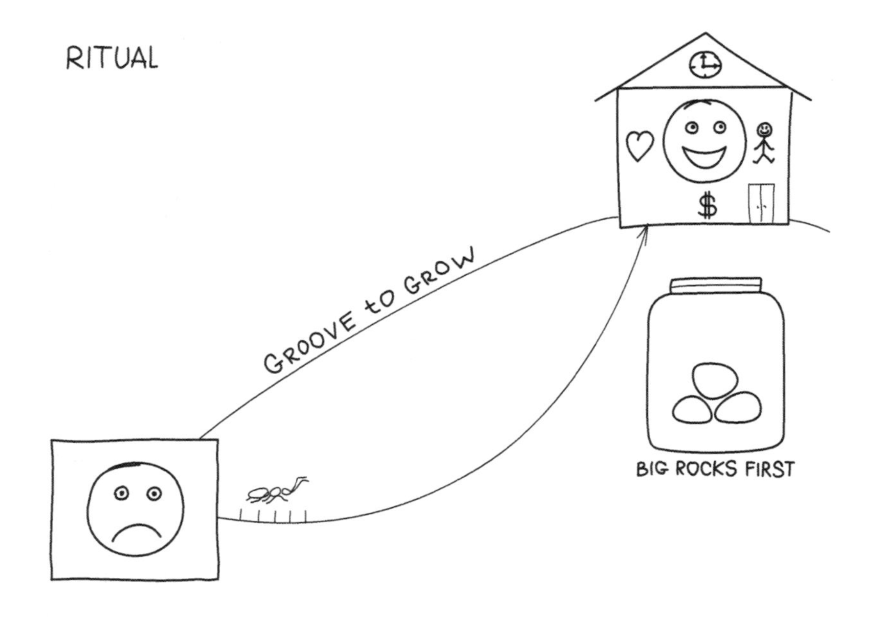

MY A-HA! MOMENT AND MY DAILY "RICH-UAL"

For most of my early years, I had no particular daily pattern. I just got up every morning and pursued my passion for writing and teaching and entrepreneurship. The car crash in 2003 changed all of that. When I came out of the coma after my car accident I had one of those A-HA!'s that people are always talking about. I remembered the story of the big rocks, and I realized that I hadn't done a very good job of putting big rocks first in my life. I thought, if God is really that important to me, then shouldn't His big rock go in the jar of my day first? And if my health is really important to me, then shouldn't I make exercise and proper nutrition fit into my schedule every day? If my marriage is important to me, shouldn't I make sure I work on it every single day? In those moments of clarity after my accident, I realized that none of these things had come first in my life. I had put the sand and the pebble things first. And that had to change. I had to put the important things—the big rocks—in first.

And then I thought to myself, what if I could turn the big rocks into habits? What if I could create a personal ritual of only big rock things that I did everyday, at the same time, in the same order?

I soon discovered that almost all great achievers have daily rituals. Their rituals vary wildly, but they all have consistent routines, habits, and regimens.

During the months of recovery that followed my accident I began to develop a personalized set of my most important habits. I even named my ritual! I called it "The Rich-ual." It's a cheesy name, but it's a way to remind myself that consistent habit is the fastest way to grow rich in ALL areas of my life. What will you name your ritual? My friend Jack Canfield calls his ritual the "Hour of Power." He meditates for twenty minutes, works out for twenty minutes, and trains his brain for twenty more.

I was flying recently and saw my friend and bestselling author, Deepak Chopra, sitting across the aisle from me. I asked him about his daily regimen. He said he rises about 3AM and meditates for two hours. Talk about your early morning ritual!

Charles Dickens had a morning ritual AND an afternoon ritual. He rose promptly at 7:00am, had eaten by 8:00, and was in his study by 9:00, writing. His afternoon ritual was lunch with his family, followed by a vigorous three-hour walk through the countryside.

I could go on and on with examples...successful people have daily rituals, and they get them done, rain or shine.

Your ritual doesn't have to follow a strict time guideline. It can be as short as a half an hour, or as long as Dickens'. The important thing is to set aside a block of time every day, fill that block with the most important actions, and make that time and that ritual sacred. Let me repeat that because it is so important. A ritual is a sacred block of time set aside, every day, and filled with your most important habits.

A true ritual is much different than just a daily "schedule." Anything can happen in a schedule. A ritual is time to get done what really matters—the big rocks. It's been said that 20% of your actions produce 80% of your results—those are the big rocks. Commit to getting them done every day.

A ritual is to successful people what a training regimen is to professional athletes. The habits of your ritual are your sit-ups, your push-ups, and your sprints. Your ritual is your workout...the "stretching" of your mind, body and spirit.

A ritual has many residual benefits. It helps you build character, courage and determination. It leads to strengthening your willpower. It helps you think deeper, rise higher and see farther. It is the essence of success.

Nothing makes my life richer and more rewarding than the big rocks I do every day. My ritual is a source of enormous personal power. Magic really happens when you take effective strategies—like meditation, or exercise—and turn them into daily habits. It's that compound interest we've been talking about! But you have to choose the right big rocks to make habits.

BUILDING YOUR PERSONAL RITUAL

One of the things in your personal ritual should be drawing the Four Maps. They are designed to be big rocks. I can't tell you exactly what your other big rocks should be—it's your personal ritual—but I've found that the most important big rock habits tend to fall into three distinct categories: Being, Body, and Brain. As you develop your own ritual, I recommend you start with at least one habit from each of these categories.

Being

Your Being—your spirit, your essence, your life force, that spark of eternity that resides in you—is so wise. I believe that the genius of your spirit is immeasurably wise, unfathomably profound, and indescribably brilliant. How do you tap into your innate genius, and into the genius of the Universe? Do you meditate, do you pray, do you go out and commune with nature, or human nature? Your life will be better if you do. Whatever you believe, choose to make some aspect of "being" a part of your daily ritual.

Body

Your body is such an amazing machine. It orchestrates all the systems of your life—breathing, digesting, elimination, circulation, immunity—without a single conscious thought on your part. Each cell of your body contains the DNA blueprint to reproduce itself indefinitely. Stem cells in your body can reproduce an entire human being from a single cell. The genius that resides in every cell of your body is unfathomable. How do you take care of it? Do you stretch, do you walk, do you lift weights or swim? Do you do Yoga or Tai-Chi? Do you eat right? You can't live an Ideal Lifestyle unless you are as healthy as you can be. Make sure one of your everyday big rocks involves taking care of your body.

Brain

Your brain is the most complex entity in the entire known universe. Everything you've ever experienced is permanently recorded in your cerebral computer. How are you treating your brain? Are you preparing for your day with enough sleep, or are you letting the whirlwind distractions keep you up late at night? Are you actively learning, or are you comfortable with what you already know? Are you reading? Are you spending time to ponder and think deeply? Do you take time to plan for your future? What can you do to fine-tune your machine? Make it a part of your ritual.

WRITE DOWN YOUR RITUAL

Hopefully, I've gotten you thinking about what exactly makes up your personal ritual. On your Ritual Map, I want you to write down what you've been thinking. To the left of the smiley face write, "My Ritual" and underneath it put, "Being," "Brain," and "Body," with a blank line next to each one. It might look like this: Your ritual will eventually encompass more than three (3) things, but we are starting slowly, so just write down three (3) things that come to mind, one for each category.

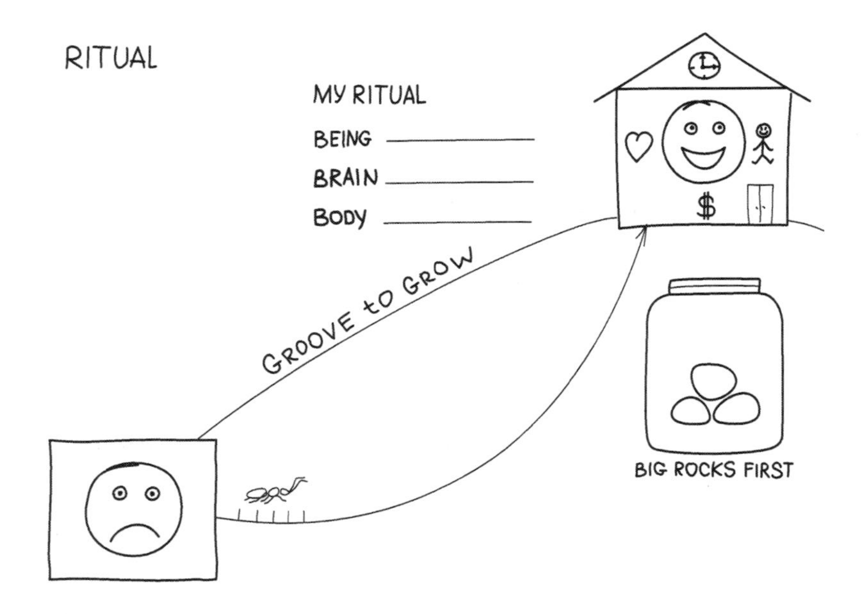

PLAN YOUR RITUAL—IT'S ABOUT TIME.

Sometimes my clients say to me, "Bob, I know what my big rocks are, but I have trouble doing them. I lack the willpower." I understand the feeling, believe me. If the big rocks were easy to do, we wouldn't need to read books like this ☺.

The great thing about fixed routines, habits, and rituals, is that you only have to make one decision—the decision to start your routine—to cover a hundred smaller decisions—all the little pieces of your routine. It's like jumping out onto a dance floor. Well, what are you going to do now? You're not just going to stand there, are you? No way, you're on a dance floor. You

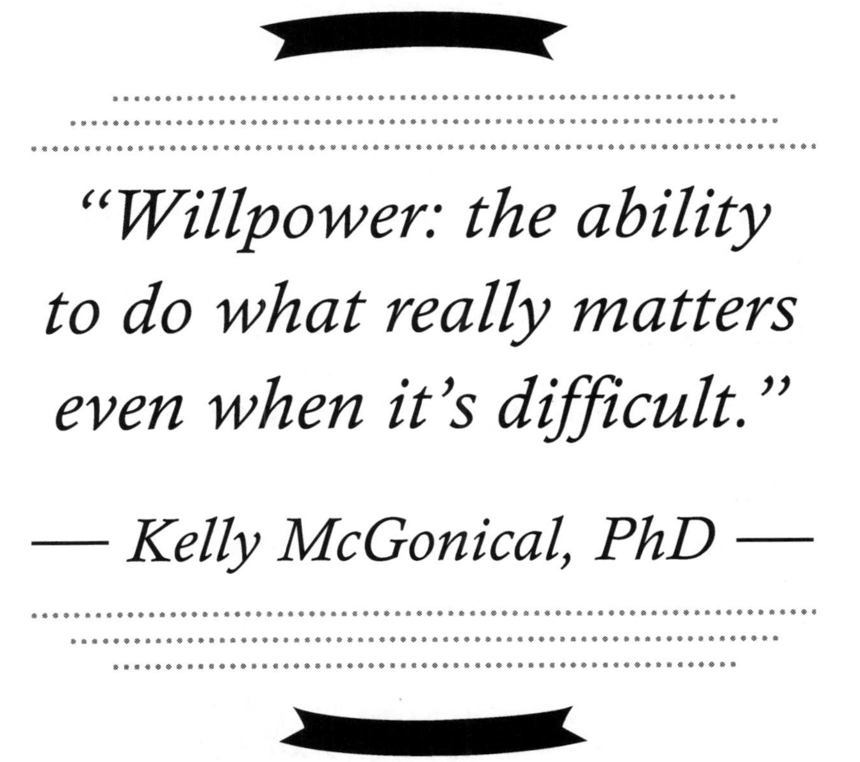
"Willpower: the ability
to do what really matters
even when it's difficult."
— Kelly McGonical, PhD —

gotta dance. Good thing you know a step-by-step dance routine. It's your ritual. So what do you do? You follow the steps that you are familiar with, and you dance. Once you make the first key decision to start your ritual, the rest is pre-determined. It's habit. You only need to find the willpower for that one decision.

My strong recommendation is to set aside a block of time every day for your ritual. It can be morning, afternoon, or evening. I do my ritual in the morning, right after I wake up. My other strong recommendation is that your ritual consists of a set number of things that never change, that you do in a specific order—everything in its place. That way, you will never have to make more than one decision to complete your ritual. You make that first key decision, and the other pieces follow like a dance routine. In case you were wondering (or needing an example), here is exactly what I do in my ritual, in order:

MY "RICH-UAL"

Being

My spiritual life means a lot to me, so I start my ritual by studying inspirational texts (usually scripture—my favorites are the Bible and the Book of Mormon) for about thirty minutes. Then I connect with my Higher Power (usually through a kneeling prayer or meditation) until I feel humbled and at peace. I use the words "Higher Power" when speaking to audiences of various spiritual beliefs (like this book) because those words fit everyone—even humanists or others who might not believe in God. I try to be sensitive enough to notice the "downloads"—the impressions I might receive—and then, afterwards, I record these special impressions in my journal.

Body

After my study I get on the treadmill in my fitness room and exercise for about thirty minutes. Sometimes I do 33 minutes and 33 seconds. Or 37 minutes and 37 seconds...Or 44 minutes and 44 seconds...just because I like those nice even numbers ☺. Sometimes I switch up and do different types of plyometric exercises, or even just stretches. You don't need an exercise room to workout, but I make sure to work on my body for at least thirty minutes.

Brain

As I'm exercising, I'm naturally thinking about my day. Sometimes I read books or record my thoughts on a voice recorded "journal" while walking. When I'm finished, I immediately sit down and begin to draw my Four Actions. This is the time where I make conscious decisions to climb towards my Ideal Lifestyle.

When I'm done, I take a shower and head into the kitchen to make myself a healthy breakfast with high power nutritionals. And that's it! My "Rich-ual" ☺. I've determined the most important things in my life—

my big rocks—and I've made them habits. I try to get them done first, every day. What's your ritual?

GROOVE TO GROW

The only thing left to do on your Ritual Map is to sign your name and make a 24-hour commitment to complete your personal ritual. But, before we finish, I want to step back and share something very important to me, what I call "The Groove."

Something miraculous happens when, day after day, you are completing your personal ritual. You start to get into a groove in your life. It's hard to explain unless you've lived it, but you become rather unstoppable. All concerns about willpower and procrastination fall away. Your life becomes a manifestation of the principle of compound interest.

You'll notice that the curve of compound interest starts up very slowly, and it's often that way when we try to build a new habit or develop a personalized ritual. It's going to be hard at first to fit that ritual time into your life. But soon, the curve goes up dramatically.

When I hear athletes talking about getting "hot" or getting into an unstoppable "zone" in reference to sporting events, I believe they are really talking about this groove. They can get into a zone because they have put years of effort into their sport, and because every day they are practicing a ritual to prepare them for success.

Look at your Ritual Map, at the phrase "Groove to Grow" that I had you write way back at the beginning. I want you to virtualize what it will feel like to be in that groove. How will it feel to have no problems with willpower? How will it feel to get done what's really important every single day? The groove is real, and you can achieve it in your own life. Are you committed to do it?

If so, sign your name and give yourself a big pat on the back. Your completed Ritual Map should look something like this:

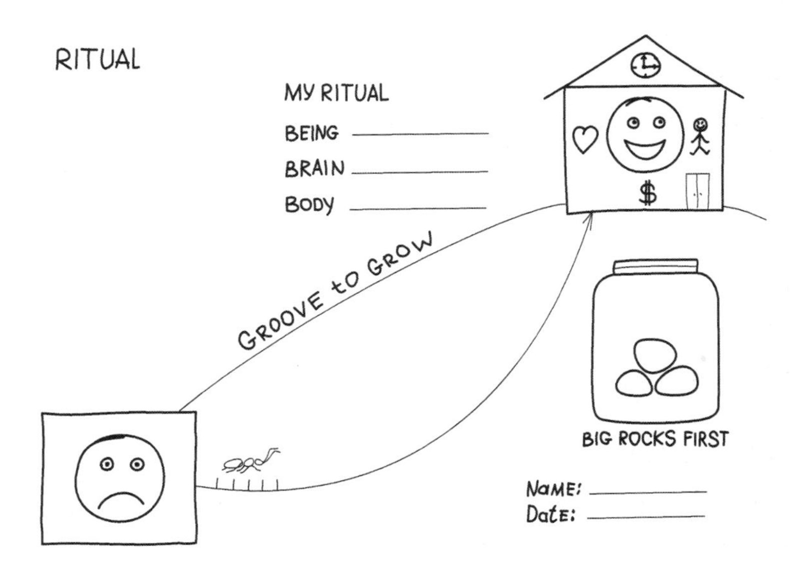

ANOTHER WAY OF VISUALIZING YOUR RITUAL

I know that was a lot to learn. The section might have seemed a little long to you, and maybe not so simple. That's okay, you are moving into more advanced techniques. Sadly, most people never develop a ritual or understand the power of compound, consistent growth. They float along through life. Even if they do develop a ritual, they often never learn to personalize it to their own values, to their own daily needs, to their own hero's journey. What you have just learned is revolutionary. It's worth the effort to learn and teach.

I've developed a quick diagram if you are more advanced, and you want to write down your ritual in more detail. You don't have to do it every day, but it might help you conceptualize your ritual. I call it the Ritual Visual:

THE RITUAL VISUAL

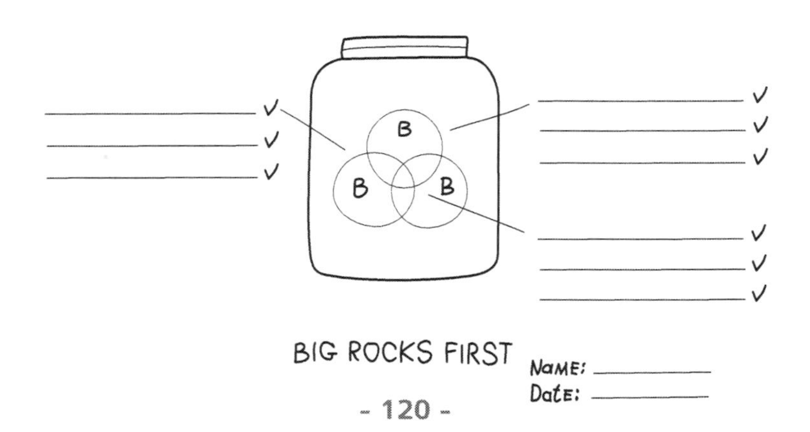

That's your big rocks jar, and inside are three overlapping circles representing your big rocks. Each is labeled with a "B" representing "Being," "Brain," and "Body." And there are places for you to write down the elements of your ritual that correlate to each of the rocks. Fill them in to plan your daily ritual.

Many of my clients choose to use this Ritual Visual as a daily checklist for their personal ritual. I advise them to still keep drawing the full Ritual Map, even if it seems repetitious. I want them to draw the curve and the ant, and be reminded of the power of compound interest. I want them to take a moment to virtualize what it will feel like to find the "Groove" and live a life full of willpower.

STEP-BY-STEP RECAP

In review, to draw your Ritual Map, here is what you need to do:

1. Draw your "before" and "after" frowny and smiley faces, and put the smiley face in the dream home, surrounded by the markers of an Ideal Lifestyle.

2. Draw the curve of compound interest and Aesop's Ant to remind you of the power of consistent, daily action.

3. Draw your "Big Rocks" Jar to remind you to do the truly important things first.

4. Write down three (3) pieces of your personal ritual, one each for "Being," "Brain," and "Body."

5. Virtualize, with all five senses, how life will feel when you find your "Groove" and are getting the important things done every day.

6. Make a 24-hour commitment to completing your personal ritual. Sign your name to demonstrate your commitment.

MAP 4 TASK

HABIT AND TASK (AGAIN)

I'VE SAID IT before and I'll say it again ☺: Every human action fits into one of two categories. It's either a repeated habit or a "one-off" task. Remember our analogy of wanting perfect teeth? In order to get those pearly whites you have to combine daily rituals (like flossing) with specific, project-oriented tasks (like a trip to the dentist for a cleaning). The pathway up the mountain to our personalized Ideal Lifestyle works the same way. Our daily success rituals take care of the big rocks, the things we've determined to make habits and permanent aspects of our character, and then we combine those habits with specific actions towards planned projects and milestones. An Ideal Lifestyle is possible when you combine habit and task effectively, with the power of your clarity behind every action.

We've spent a lot of time in this book dealing with mindset and habit, but in the Task Map we're going to step out into the day—into the "big, bad world"—and get things done! What I'm about to teach you is a way to identify your short, medium, and long-term projects, and organize your daily tasks so that every step you take, every day, is moving you closer to your Ideal Lifestyle. This is enlightened, visual project management.

Most corporate project management is done using logical tools such as spreadsheets and strategic plans. For a lot of people (especially me) this technical way of doing things just doesn't work. I want to bring my imagination into play! I want to draw!

In the Task Map, we're not only going to write down today's tasks, we're going to draw them in context of the overall plan, backed up by the power of our purpose and reasons. It's all going to come together in the "real world."

TASK MANAGEMENT IS MUCH MORE IMPORTANT THAN TIME MANAGEMENT

Before we jump into the Task Map itself, I want to share with you some of my thoughts about effective tasks. The truth is that each day in your life is a blank canvas, and the decisions you fill it with are the brushstrokes. What sort of painting are you making with your day? Is it a success or a failure? Is it a focused masterpiece, or a chaos of random color?

In the 1980's and 90's there was a famous PBS show called "The Joy of Painting," hosted by Bob Ross. It's still often seen in reruns. I used to love to watch "The Joy of Painting," mostly because of Ross. He would say something like, "now we're going to draw a happy little tree," and then he'd make what looked like a random smudge of color on the canvas. I would think to myself, *there's no way that random smudge of color is eventually going to be part of a detailed tree. No way.* But Bob Ross knew what he was doing. He had a plan, and he kept making his seemingly random smudges. Then, suddenly, all those smudges would magically combine, and a tree would appear. It was always amazing to see that happen. It felt like a miracle. But it wasn't a miracle, and it wasn't chance—it was Bob Ross. He was in control—he knew the purpose of each and every brushstroke and where they fit in the overall plan. He could see the end from the beginning, even if I couldn't.

The tasks we choose to fill the blank canvas of our day need to be as targeted as Bob Ross' brushstrokes. From the infinite whirlwind of things we could do today, we need to identify the things we must do. But that's easier said than done when the whirlwind is swirling all around us. Here are three secrets for choosing the right tasks:

EFFECTIVE TASK SECRET #1: APPLY THE BIG PICTURE FILTER

Most of this book has been focused on helping you expand your perspective to see the big picture behind everything in your life—from your attitudes, to your "wants," and even to your champions and challenges. Why?

When you have the big picture clear in your mind, it makes identifying the right decisions much easier.

If you're applying the big picture filter to your tasks, you'll ask yourself, before you take any action: *Will this task lead me toward or away from what I really, really want?*

Make no mistake, not all the tasks you could choose today are actual steps up the mountain to your Ideal Lifestyle. Some are sideways diversions, and some are just plain backwards.

It's so much easier to choose effective tasks when you have the big picture in front of you. They just become obvious. It's like turning on a light in a dark room. The unimportant, whirlwind tasks (that would otherwise clutter your day) skitter away like insects under the light of your purpose.

EFFECTIVE TASK SECRET #2: YOU CAN ONLY CHOOSE THREE

The modern world is full of so many possibilities, and the things you can add to your Ideal Lifestyle are just as limitless. But you'll notice throughout the Four Maps we've been making lists of only three things—three wants, three reasons, three champions, three challenges, and so on.

Modern life often demands that we be good at dozens of things at once, but if we're trying to grow, we need to stay focused. If we try to improve everything at once, we can easily be paralyzed by the amount of work required. The secret to getting things done, even things as large as our Ideal Lifestyle, is to limit ourselves and focus our efforts.

Once a year, while Steve Jobs was at Apple, he took 100 of his most valuable employees on a retreat. The purpose of this retreat was to decide what revolution Apple was going to perform next. For a few years there, it seemed every project Jobs worked on at Apple ended up amazing. During the course of the retreat, he would ask his employees to give him their best ideas, and, at the very end, he put the ten best up on a whiteboard. I imagine that every one of the things on that list could have changed the world. These were some of the greatest minds at one of the greatest companies on earth. But, Jobs would walk up to the whiteboard at the end and cross out the bottom seven ideas on the list and say, "We can only do these three."

He knew that they would only have so much energy to invest in a year. If they let their energy be divided in too many directions, they would end up with mediocre products.

The genius of Jobs at Apple was the discipline to say no to the thousands of products they could market, and to focus on being "insanely great" at just a few.

So it is with your day. There are thousands of things you could do. But only a few will create lasting greatness. If you dissipate your energy into too many things you'll likely end up with a mediocre day, and, eventually, a mediocre life. The key to success is limiting yourself and dominating within your chosen boundaries. After you have mastered one area, expand to new boundaries. Divide and conquer life, one area at a time. We're not going to make exhaustive lists of things to do in the Task Map—we're going to choose three tasks and master them.

EFFECTIVE TASK SECRET #3: LOSE THE TO-DO LIST

Most people go about getting things done by use of a traditional to-do list, but to-do lists are the opposite of efficiency. In fact, a to-do list is the worst life management tool ever invented, because it's designed to reinforce the completion of useless tasks. I recommend you take your outdated to-do list and scrap it. Yup! Crumple it up and toss it into the garbage.

Let's examine how an average Joe compiles his daily to-do list. He might begin by pondering—*Let's see... what do I need to do today*? His mind comes up with dozens of items, all seemingly equal in importance, and he jots them down. Now he's ready to get some of them done. So he scans down the list. *Let's see...what can I cross off this list quickly?* he asks himself. He starts doing the easy tasks—because they're fast and easy to cross off. And then, something interesting happens. Each time he crosses something off his list, he gets a rush of happiness. It feels good to get things done, even unimportant things. Your body is actually releasing dopamine every time you cross something off. It's a principle we'll spend much more time on at the end of this chapter, when we'll turn it around and use it for good. But, for now, back to our average Joe and his to-do list. He looks for the next easiest thing to cross off the list...and then the next easiest...and then the next, because each time he crosses something off he gets another fun surge of commitment-induced dopamine.

Be honest, have you ever reviewed your to-do list when the day is almost finished and remembered something you did but forgot to write down? Did you immediately write it down and then cross it off just to get that "to-do rush"? I knew it ☺. You're addicted! We've all been there.

You can become addicted to the act of crossing something off, even if the thing you are crossing off is not an effective task—just one of the things you "could" do, and not something you "must" do. The things we "must" do are often the hardest things to tackle. Tackle them first and procrastinate everything else.

The truth is we only have so much "task" energy in a day (even if you are much younger than me). If we don't choose essential tasks and do them first, then, at the end of the day, the important stuff is still undone. Maybe we rationalize and push it off to tomorrow's list when we'll "be fresher" (Wink, wink). But tomorrow, the cycle is repeated and the very tasks that will get us everything we've ever wanted are left undone. This is a sad recipe for how life can become overwhelmed with lots of little things—little things that in the overall picture won't even amount to a hill of beans—let alone the summit of your Ideal Lifestyle! It would be funny if it weren't so tragic.

And, what's worse, the important tasks that we've left undone sit in the back of our minds and color our personal interaction the rest of the day, no matter how many small things we've crossed off our list. Do you know what I'm talking about? You keep procrastinating the important things and then you start to worry about them. And then your worry keeps you from doing fun activities because you have "things to do"...or it makes you grumpy with your loved ones...or it keeps you from really enjoying the moments of your day...which leads to a sad life, because what is life but a collection of moments and days?

But let's focus on the positive. Let's not be fear-based. On the flipside, an incredible joy and freedom comes into your life if you use your energy to tackle the important things first. Life is amazing after the important things get done! Your day is yours and anything is possible.

THE TASK MAP

Now that I've hopefully made a few things clear about effective tasks, let's draw your Task Map. This Map will help you identify the essential things in your life, and give you a daily map to a whole new psychology for "getting things done."

Take out a pen and paper or your favorite digital device and, just like the other Maps, draw the frowny face in the limiting lifestyle, and the smiley face in the house of the Ideal Lifestyle. Draw the mountain slope connecting the two. Along that slope, I want you to write "As Good As Done!" That's our theme for this map, and you'll soon see why.

So far, your drawing might look like this:

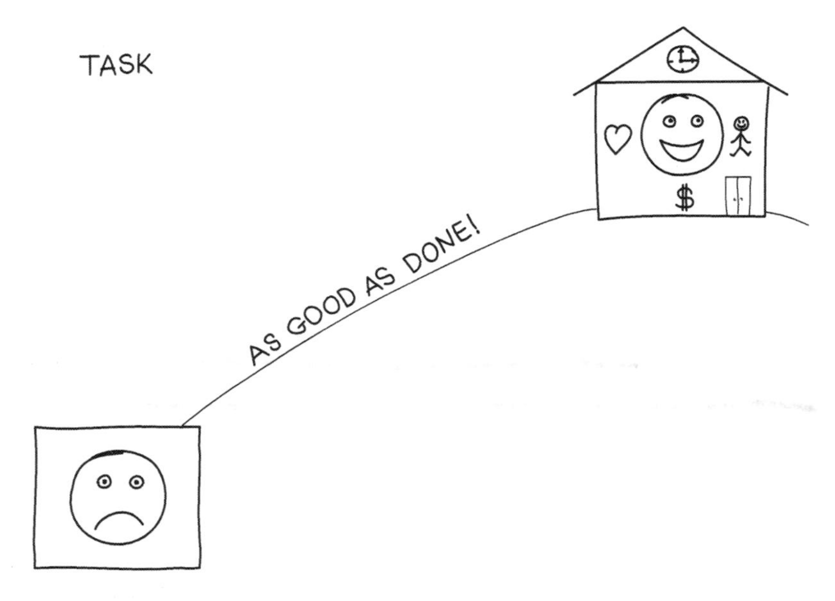

Next, we're going to draw the principle of "you can only choose three" on your Task Map. I want you to draw a triangle in the upper left hand corner, like a funnel, and above the funnel write "100" and then below the funnel write "3." Out of hundreds of things you could do today, you can only be really great at three (3). It might look something like this:

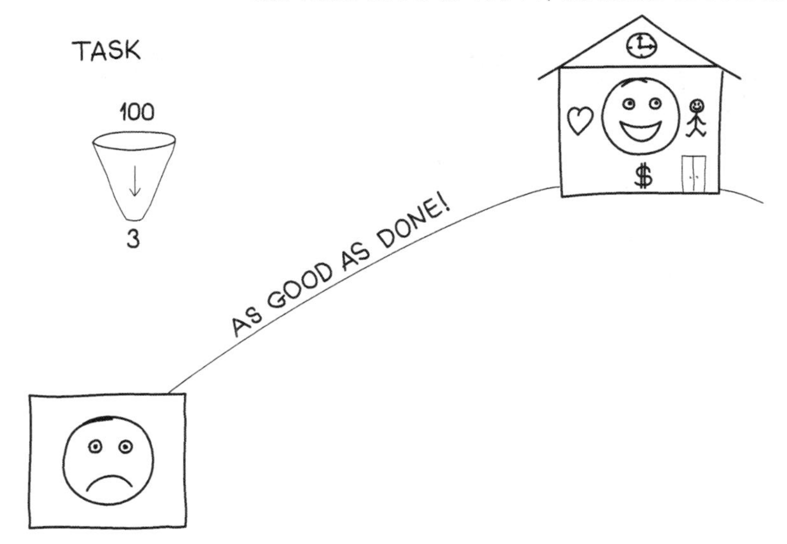

Looking good. Now we're going to divide the space under the slope into three (3) sections. Under the first section, I want you to write "Now." Under the second, "1 Year," and under the third, "5 Years." It should look like this:

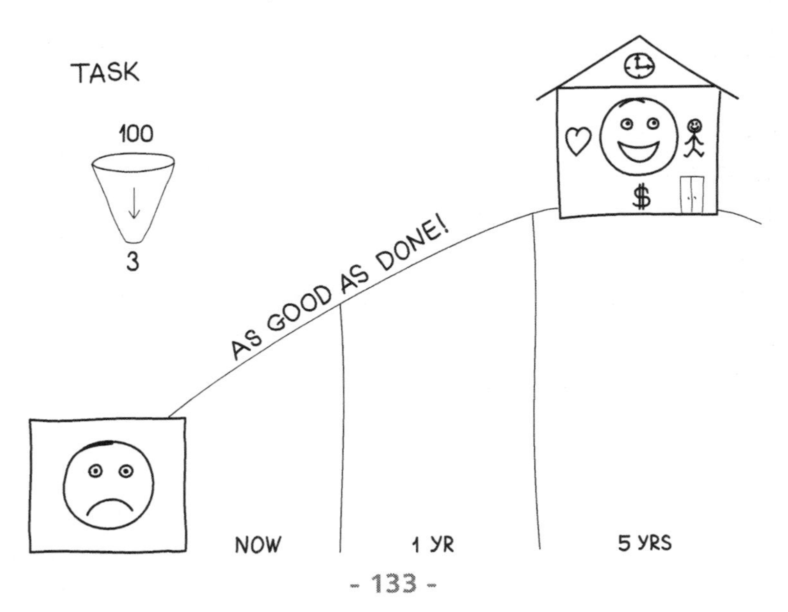

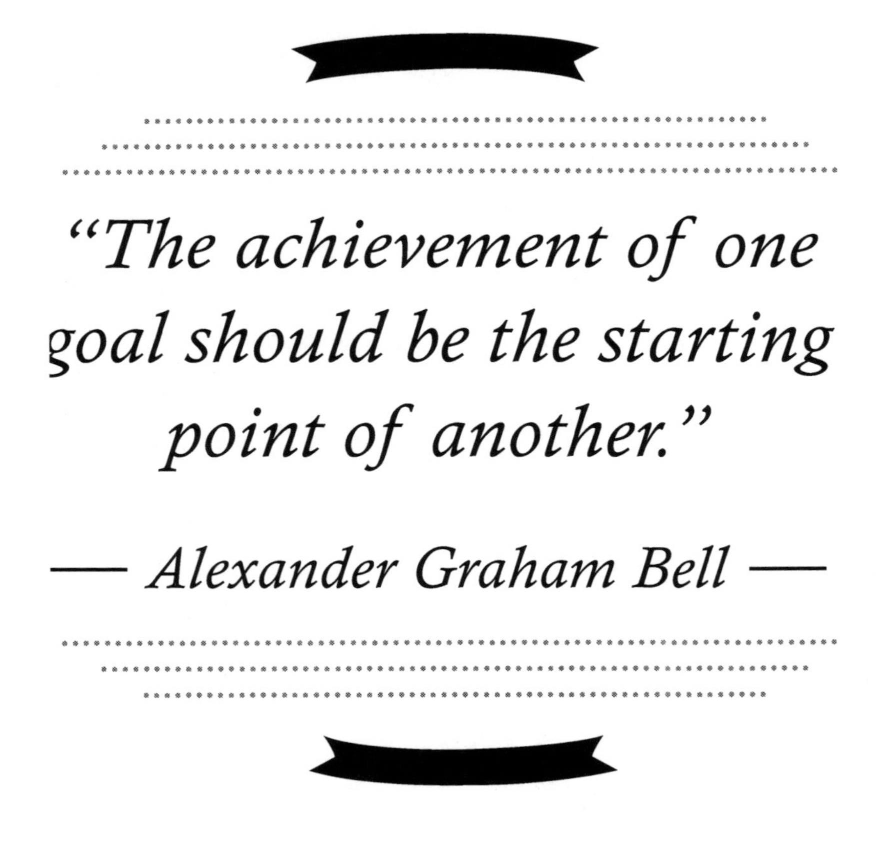
"The achievement of one goal should be the starting point of another."
— Alexander Graham Bell —

Time is passing as you climb up the mountain to your Ideal Lifestyle. Just as you are building towards the greatest life you can possibly imagine, every one of your tasks should be building towards larger and larger objectives.

Let's give each of the three (3) sections of our Task Map a unique name. As we go along, we're going to talk about these names individually and in much more depth, because my names are different than anything you'll find in normal project management.

In the space to the far right, under the dream home, I want you to write the word "Ideals." In the middle I want you to write the word "Dones," and in the left space I want you to write the word "Musts." It might look something like this:

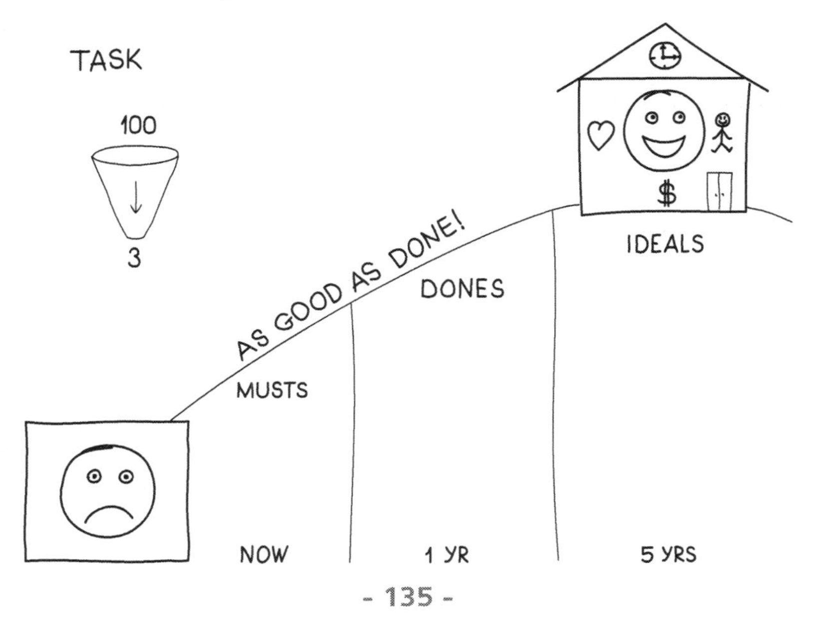

Ideals are long-term projects with a 5-year time horizon.

Dones are intermediate projects with up to a one-year time horizon.

Musts are today's absolutely essential tasks.

Ideals

Let's start with Ideals. As my mentor Stephen Covey said, "Begin with the end in mind." You have big dreams in life. We've been writing them down throughout the Four Maps. Remember on your Clarity Map, all the things you desperately wanted to add to your life? You virtualized living your Ideal Lifestyle and wrote out three aspects of it. Then you wrote out powerful motivating reasons. Maybe your reasons were so strong that you labeled them the very "purpose" of your life. Now is the time to take the work you did on your Clarity Map and turn your three "wants" into concrete objectives to be completed within a 5-year timeframe.

On your Task Map, I want you to write three lines under the "Ideals" section of the mountain. It should look like this:

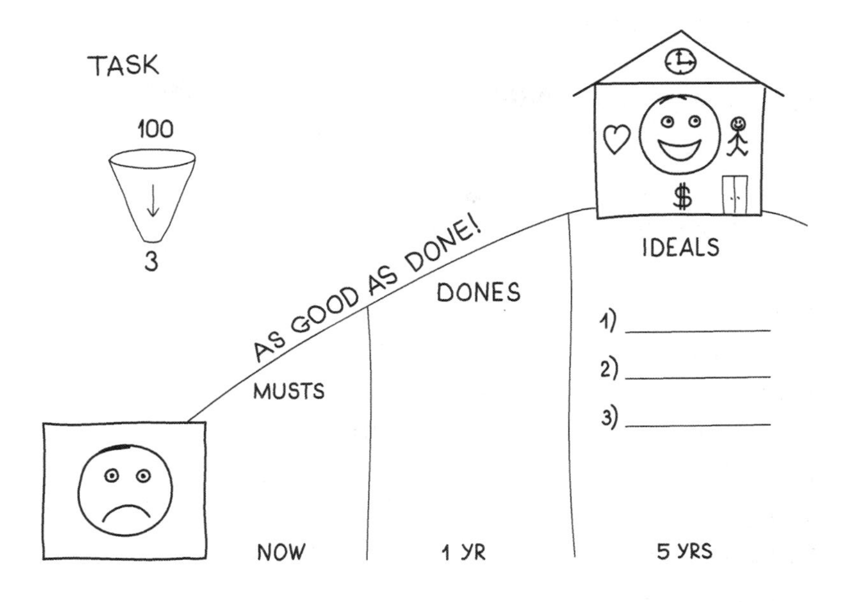

You may think five years is too long a horizon, but these three Ideals are enormous objectives. We're talking here about huge aspects of your dream lifestyle.

For example, if one of the markers of your Ideal Lifestyle is having complete financial freedom (there's a reason you've been drawing a $ sign on every single one of the Four Maps) then a good 5-year Ideal might be starting and selling a company, or owning a few apartment units.

If one of the markers of your Ideal Lifestyle is having a life full of loving relationships, then one of your 5-year Ideals could be finding that special someone.

If the concept is still confusing, I want you to imagine being interviewed in five years. The interviewer asks you what you are most proud of accomplishing. What would you answer? If you were born to write that novel, did you write it? If you were born to be an entrepreneur, did you launch a successful business? If you were born to solve a world problem, did you figure out how to fund that non-profit and solve it?

I urge you to get as specific as possible with these Ideals. Although it's great to say, "I'm going to be a super athlete," it's far more effective to select a specific marker of superstardom, like, "I'm going to compete in three triathlons." You can get specific, even if we're talking about Ideals five years into the future.

I'll give you an example from my own life:

As I complete my Clarity Map and "virtualize" my Ideal Lifestyle, I always come back to a strong desire to help other people grow. It's one of my three "wants" every time. It's the purpose of my life.

That's why one of my Task Map Ideals is to publish 25 (25!) short books in the next five years. My son Aaron and I have dozens of ideas for powerful, to-the-point transformative books, and I'm in love with new online methods of distribution. We're calling our company

"LittleBetter Books," and we're very excited. Here is how I write my Ideal on my Task Map:

"I Have 25! Transformative books available for download online!"

It took me 35 years to write my first 10 books, so creating 25 books in the next 5 years is a big Ideal! It's going to take a lot of work, enormous focus, and probably every single minute of the next five years.

Are you clear on what an Ideal is? Remember, you can only choose three. If you have more than three major projects on your plate at once, they all suffer. You only have so much time and energy. Choose only Ideals that you really, really, want.

Also, these Ideals aren't likely to change much for the next FIVE YEARS. So they had better be things you are excited about accomplishing.

Take a deep breath and write down your three Ideals.

Dones

A Done (I like to write it as "Done!") is an intermediate project that leads directly towards one of your Ideals. Think of your Dones as the milestones you pass on your way to the top of the mountain. A Done can take you anywhere from a month to a year to accomplish, and you'll need to stack up more than a few of them to reach your 5-year Ideal.

On your Task Map, I want you to write three (3) lines under the Dones section of the mountain. It should look like this:

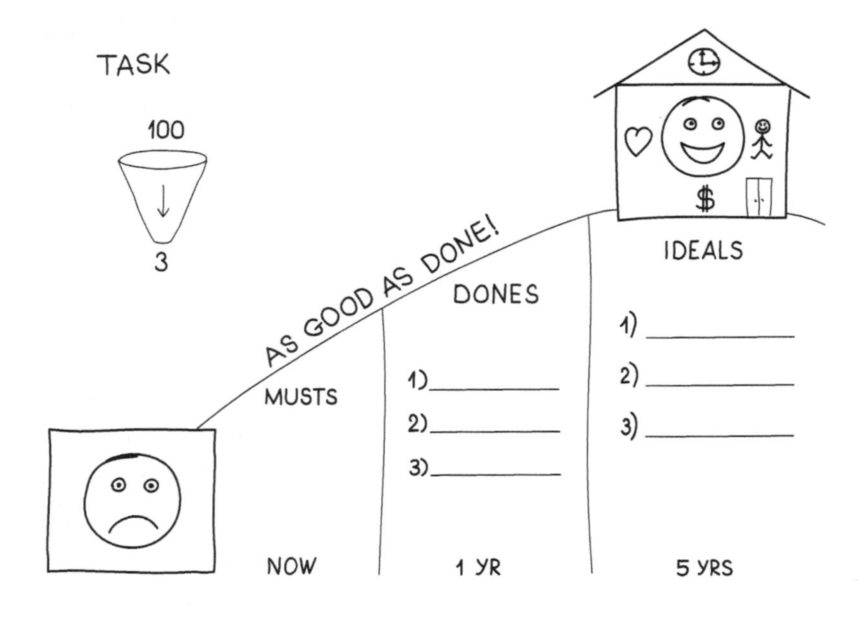

FLIP THE DONE! SWITCH.

I bet you're wondering by now why I call these intermediate projects Dones and not something like "Goals"?

It all has to do with the way your brain responds to "past" vs. "future" thinking. It turns out there's a huge difference in our brains between a goal and a Done!

Everybody says, "set goals" but the way most people approach their goals causes more harm than good. They set goals that aren't urgent, that don't have any commitment behind them, like New Year's resolutions—a wishy-washy type of thinking. Nothing is at stake. And when nothing is at stake, success doesn't happen.

There's a switch you need to flip in your mind. The switch is from "hoping to do it" to "having done it." I call it the "Done! Switch."

I always write my Ideals and Dones in the past tense, as if I've *already* done it. You're retraining yourself to think from that area in your mind where things might never happen, to a place where they have already happened. It's a Jedi mind trick on yourself, and it has a measurable effect on your brain and your willpower.

When you declare something as "Done!" instead of hoping for it as a goal, it suddenly becomes a matter of personal integrity to actually get it done. Your word is on the line. I think we all want to be people who, when we speak our word, it's done. We want to be the type of person that others can count on.

HOW DONES BUILD TO IDEALS

Each one of your three Ideals is going need lots of these different Done projects. If this is your first time completing the Task Map, I recommend taking some time to brainstorm (on a separate list) the Dones for each of your three 5-year Ideals. You're going to have an entirely different list of Dones for each Ideal.

I have a long list of Dones over the next year to achieve my Ideal of Publishing 25 books. Here are a few examples:

> Finish This Book!
>
> Oversee editing and formatting of The Four Maps.
>
> Finish final edits on my next book, tentatively titled, 10 Minutes to a Great Idea.
>
> Write 5 Newsletters for my fans.
>
> Recruit a "Launch Team" of reviewers to get feedback on each book.
>
> Oversee the creation of a new Robertallen.com.

It's a long list...and getting longer. But I don't write out every one of my Dones everyday. That would be overwhelming.

Timing is crucial. Some of your Done projects are essential right now, they need to get Done! If you look at my list, I can't do certain Dones until other ones are completed. I can't oversee the editing of this book until this book is finished ☺.

If you apply the big picture filter, the essential Dones will jump out at you. For me and my 25 books Ideal, I have to finish this chapter.

When I get up in the morning and draw out my Task Map, I write one simple sentence to remind me of the next Done for my Ideal Publishing Project, and I make sure to put it in the past tense:

"I've finished my book The Four Maps of Happy, Successful People"

Take a deep breath and think about a specific Done project for each of the three Ideals on your Task Map. Of the hundred intermediate projects you could focus on today, which ones scream at you as being real, substantive, possible, essential? Commit to them as "Done!" and write them down.

Musts

Now you've committed to your Ideals and your Dones. If you're like me, then you've probably publicized your Dones to your friends and family, so you have some social motivation to help you keep your word. The rubber is finally on the road. Your day stretches out. If you are going to make your Ideal Lifestyle a reality, you *must* get things done.

A Must is an effective daily task that builds towards a Done. Think of them as all the footsteps you take as you climb a mountain. A Done, like writing a book, is a longer-term project. A Must is short term—like getting down 500 words today. No words, no book. You can't have Ideals without Dones, and you certainly can't reach your Dones without hundreds of Musts.

On your Task Map, I want you to write three (3) lines under the Musts section of the mountain. It should look like this:

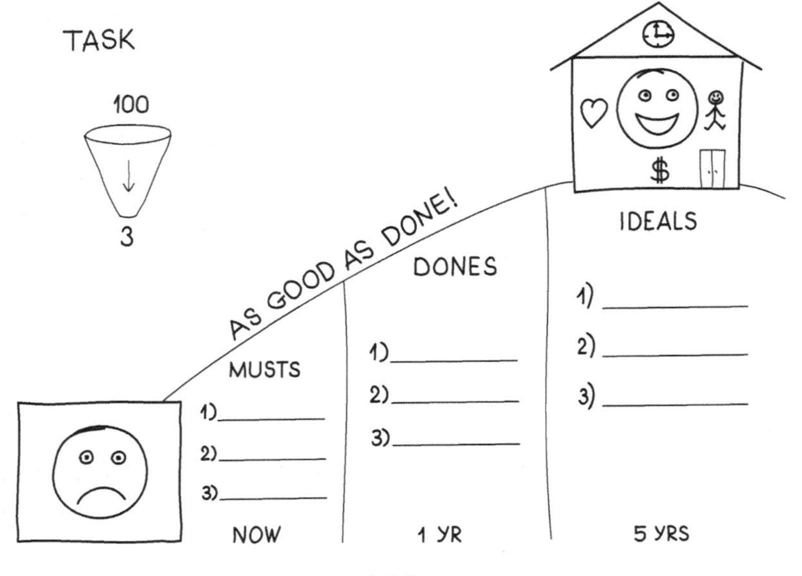

It might seem crazy to have only three Musts on your entire Task Map. I can hear you saying, "are you really teaching me Bob that I replace my 100 item to-do list with only three Musts?"

That's exactly what I'm saying. There is enormous power in limiting your tasks. If you could only do three things today to reach your Ideal Lifestyle, what would you do?

Those are your Musts. They are more important than laundry, more important than email or social media, more important than a thousand other tasks. They are absolutely essential tasks. When you complete them, your life will improve dramatically. We'll talk more at the end of this section about exactly how finishing your Musts changes your brain and your life, but for now, I want you to fill those three (3) lines with your three Musts, one for each Done project.

When you have finished, I want you to sign and date the bottom of your Task Action. You're committed for the day. Now give yourself a big pat on the back, and go out into your day and get things DONE!

THE SUCCESS PYRAMID

I realize I just taught you a lot. A lot of new words and maybe some pretty tough concepts. I've created a way to visualize the Musts—Dones—Ideals concept I've just taught you. I call it the Success Pyramid. Give it a gander:

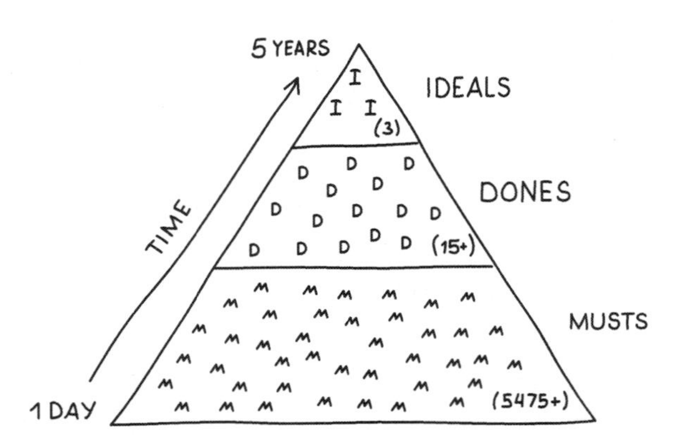

Small daily tasks (Musts) flow up into mid-range projects (Dones) and these flow up into specific lifestyle attributes (Ideals.) If you "only choose three" and do three essential Musts every day, and three Dones every year, you will end up doing at least 5475 Musts and 15 Dones before you reach your three Ideals. In reality you will probably end up doing far more Musts and Dones to reach your Ideals. Make sense?

If you're a verbal learner, here is a sentence that lays out the process:

You *must* get things *done* to reach your *ideals*.

Musts to Dones to Ideals. That's the flow of success. There are no shortcuts. Just like the little ant from the Ritual Map, you have to take consistent action.

WHAT TO DO WHEN YOU FINISH YOUR MUSTS

The first question I get when I teach people the Task Map is, "what happens after I finish my three Musts?" We live in a society that often requires enormous amounts of work. And that's okay. I only want you to choose three Musts at a time (I'll share the reason for that very soon), but it's possible to finish dozens of Musts in the same day—if you do it the right way. After you finish your three Musts, here's what I suggest. The answer has two key parts, and both are incredibly important:

1. Take a deep breath to Celebrate.

Life happens moment to moment. Any chance we have to give ourselves some happiness is a chance we should take. It's an enormous accomplishment to complete your Musts in a day. You didn't choose things that were easy to do. You chose essential tasks. Even if you are under enormous deadlines, three Musts a day is "enough," over time, to reach your Ideal Lifestyle. If you decide to keep going and doing more Musts, remember what you've already accomplished, and don't let that positive feeling get away from you. That positive feeling is part of your Ideal Lifestyle! If you ignore the celebration and move on anxiously to new tasks, you're missing the point of this book (and life!).

2. Take inventory of your energy, and, if you're ready, commit to three more Musts.

Let's assume you finish your ritual, and then you finish your Musts, your essential tasks, soon afterwards. You've had an A+ morning. If you decide you have more energy, simply go back to your Task Action, look at your Ideals and your Dones again, and write down three more Musts.

But don't write down anything you aren't absolutely willing to commit to. And don't do anything unless you have written it down first.

I know that sounds rigid or even crazy, but the reason is dopamine. Keeping commitments is a drug. When you commit to do something and do it, your body releases a feel-good drug. It's a natural high. And if you write that thing down before you do it, your body releases more dopamine.

When you keep a commitment, even if it is one you made with yourself only five seconds before, there is a scientifically measurable effect on your happiness. You can literally make yourself happy by making and keeping small commitments.

You don't miss a paycheck at your job, do you? Why would you pass up on the chance to get some happiness injected into your brain?

Try it out. Write on your Task Map, "I'm going to walk across the room." and then walk across the room. Write, "I'm going to finish reading this chapter" and then finish the chapter. I believe you'll feel better. What's recorded is rewarded.

I believe every human wants to be a commitment keeper. It's universally ingrained in us. This is why it feels good to check off even the useless tasks of a typical to-do list. If you finish your three musts, and you have a lot of energy leftover, by all means do more.

But, I don't want you to do useless tasks, which is why every time you choose new Musts in a day, I'm asking you to choose only three. That way you'll always be looking at a larger list of possibilities and singling out effective, essential tasks.

I also don't want you to fail to accomplish your three Musts, whether they are the first set of three for your day, or the fifth set. I want you to go to bed with the feeling of hope and accomplishment that comes from keeping a commitment to yourself and to others. So make sure, if you decide to go for more, that you commit to getting them Done!

I would also urge you to stay on target with your Musts. Another problem with the modern lifestyle is something I like to call "task drift." You start on one thing, and you soon realize there are other tasks waiting on the periphery. Maybe one of your Musts is to research a crucial website or marketing strategy, but invariably, because the Internet is full of every type of information, your research leads you to other interesting sites and strategies. If you don't have a fixed set of Musts, you're liable to wander off and do things that don't contribute directly to your Dones and Ideals. You might learn a lot, but you won't get anything done. I know from personal experience that without clear Musts I can get lost in task-drift for hours. Musts serve as lighthouses in the fog of information, to bring me back to essential tasks. If I find something truly interesting, I can make it a Must for tomorrow. But, when I'm in the middle of a Must, I always try to stay on target until the task is completed.

WHEN YOU COMMIT, GOOD THINGS HAPPEN

Back in the Anticipation Map, I encouraged you to write down your daily Champions, because when you recognize your champions and anticipate good things, good things tend to happen. I want to come back to that concept here, at the close of the Task Map, because it's so very important. There is a great quote on Commitment that has been around for many decades. WH Murray, a

WWII prison-camp survivor and Scottish Mountaineer wrote it in his 1951 book, *The Scottish Himalayan Expedition*. You might have heard it before, but this time I want you to really ponder it, because it contains a powerful truth:

"This may sound too simple but is great in consequence: Until one is committed there is hesitancy, the chance to draw back, always ineffectiveness. Concerning all acts of initiative (and creation) there is one elementary truth, the ignorance of which kills countless ideas and splendid plans: That the moment one definitely commits oneself, then providence moves too. All sorts of things occur to help one that would never otherwise have occurred. A whole stream of events issues from the decision, raising in one's favor all manner of unforeseen incidents and meetings and material assistance, which no man could have dreamt would have come his way. I have learned a deep respect for one of Goethe's couplets:

> Whatever you can do, or dream you can, begin it.
> Boldness has genius, power and magic in it."

Depending on your religious beliefs, "providence" in this quote can mean many things. It can mean God, or other champions, like friends, or even things like economies, and markets.

My life has taught me that commitment is powerful, and it's infectious. The Universe will join in and help you reach your goals. Make the commitment today to reach your Ideals, fill your day up with Musts, and watch what happens.

STEP-BY-STEP RECAP

In review, to draw your Task Map, here is what you need to do:

1. Draw your "before" and "after" frowny and smiley faces, and put the smiley face in the dream home, surrounded by the markers of an Ideal Lifestyle.

2. Draw your path up the mountain and break it into three (3) sections, representing 5 years, 1 year, and right now.

3. Write down three (3) of your 5-year Ideals.

4. Write down three (3) Dones—short or mid-term projects that build towards your 5-year Ideals.

5. Write down three (3) of today's Musts—specific tasks that build towards your Dones.

6. To illustrate the principle of "We Can Only Choose Three," draw (in the top left) a funnel with "100" going in and "3" coming out.

7. Make a commitment to completing your day's Musts within the next 24 hours. Sign your name to indicate your commitment.

8. Trust the power of bold action and Virtualize, with all five senses, how, now that you've committed, your champions will come out of the woodwork to help you.

PART THREE:
TRANSFORMATION

YOU WERE BORN TO DO GREAT THINGS

THE FOUR MAPS is a transformative book. Transformation implies growth, change, and metamorphosis. My hope is that this book is your catalyst to escape the limited, caterpillar life you might be living and claim the limitless, butterfly inheritance of your Ideal Lifestyle.

Let's take a bird's eye overview of what we have learned together:

I've tried to fit the lessons of my entire life into just four diagrams. I wrote this book so that whenever you ask yourself, "How can I have a successful life?" you would immediately think of the Four Maps as an answer.

If you complete each of the Four Maps every day, I believe you will become an unstoppably successful person, inside and out.

It would be wonderful, but none of us has the time each day to read entire books about personal growth. I tried to make the Four Maps compact enough that the diagrams could do the psychological work of an entire book in less than fifteen minutes of drawing. At the same time, I wanted to make the drawings so simple—so easy to create—that you could teach them to a child.

I also tried to make each of the Maps memorable, so that whenever you find yourself overwhelmed or depressed or angry about life, you could go back to square one. You could start with a "before" picture of your frowny face life and imagine a better life outside the walls of fear. The walls are imaginary. The fears are paper tigers. All it takes to change your life is one step up the mountain towards a smiley-face life. You can do that right now. Nothing is stopping you from taking that first step.

The Clarity Map invites you to peer through the fog of doubt and "virtualize" a new life. It asks:

"What do you really want and why do you want it?"

The Anticipation Map expands your awareness of the inevitable challenges and the invisible champions along your hero's journey:

"What will try to stop you, and who is here to help you?"

"Ultimately, we know deeply that the other side of every fear is a freedom."

— Marilyn Ferguson —

The Ritual Map reminds you that winners have daily rituals, patterns, habits, and ceremonies. Rituals build willpower—which is the ultimate skill:

"What do you have to accomplish every day to be your best self?"

Finally, the Task Map challenges you to bring your Ideal Lifestyle into the practical world, and make a roadmap for what must get done:

"What projects will lead to your Ideal Lifestyle, and what must you do, NOW, to get them done?"

Wherever you are in life, the Four Maps are tools to unlock the life of your dreams.

Now, one final thought in conclusion:

WHY STRIVE FOR YOUR IDEAL LIFESTYLE?

In my late twenties, with my life ahead of me, all I could see were my dreams. They were very personal and often very selfish. I wanted what I wanted.

I wanted to be a millionaire. Done. I wanted a *New York Times* bestseller. Done. I wanted to drive hot car. Done. I wanted a dream house. Done.

I was very "I" focused. Me, me, me.

But, along the way I discovered, as I'm sure you will (or maybe already have), that the thrill of these personal assets and accomplishments didn't last for very long. As soon as I climbed one success mountain there was always another one off in the distance. As soon as I bought a fast car, there was always a faster one. *Five years of focus for five minutes of fun? Is this all there is to life?*

One day I woke up. I realized that I was less excited by my own successes than I was by the success stories of my students and readers. I would get an email from a successful reader and it would absolutely make my day. It wasn't just fun, it was joy. And this joy wasn't temporary—it lasted.

As I explained in the Clarity Map chapter, my Me Reasons began to fade. My We Reasons started to expand. I'm almost embarrassed today to admit that being a millionaire was actually important to me at one time in my life. It seems so "last century" to me now.

Yes, Me reasons can be fun. Exciting. Things to put on our bucket list—what we want to do before we die.

But, We reasons are what make us want to live—every day. Not things to cross off our lists but things that make every breath worth breathing.

Maybe it's an age thing—as we get older this gradual Me to We transformation takes place. Maybe, as we get ready to step into eternity, we want to leave a legacy, a gift that can keep on giving long after our hearts stop beating. I guess that's where I'm at.

Make no mistake—I encourage you to pursue your dreams, whatever they are. But I believe you were born to do great things, for yourself and for the world. Ideally, you'll come to believe that you are here to deliver a gift. Ideally, you'll find your purpose, that "We" reason, and every day you'll work like crazy to deliver it.

When you direct your passions and talents towards helping those around you, you will have limitless energy. You'll never get tired as you climb the mountain to your Ideal Lifestyle.

May you climb with a smile on your face ☺.

My best to you, now and in the wonderful future,

Bob Allen

EXPANDING YOUR KNOWLEDGE

THANKS SO MUCH for reading *The Four Maps of Happy, Successful People!* One of the things I hear a lot from my students after they learn the Four Maps is, "Bob, you could take any one of these concepts and write a book on it. You could write a book on the importance of habit, you could write a book on purpose."

I probably could, but the truth is that people far more intelligent than me have already written amazing, in-depth, science-based books about many of these topics. Like I said at the beginning, I'm not the only person with a passion for personal development.

I wrote this book in a deliberately simple style. I didn't stop much to elaborate or prove my points, even if I was talking about concepts, like the importance of habit, that could fill book after book.

The goal of the Four Maps is to get you to take action. My life has taught me that we normally do far too much studying before we dive in. The best way to learn is to do.

But every concept I shared in the Four Maps is a part of a much larger conversation about happiness and efficient living. Hopefully the Four Maps, simple as they are, can serve as "jumping off" points for your lifelong study of how to live better.

If you want to learn more, here is a short list of my favorite books on the subjects covered in the Four Maps. I've broken them down by category. By no means is this an exhaustive list, but, if you feel on fire to learn more, dive in!

You can also see this list, as well as all the diagrams from this book, on the four maps website at:

www.thefourmaps.com

The Clarity Map

Here are some great books to help you discover what you want, find your purpose, and clarify your reasons:

A Whole New Mind: Why Right-Brainers Will Rule the Future, by Daniel H. Pink

Switch: How to Change Things where Change is Hard, by Chip Heath and Dan Heath

Spontaneous Fulfillment of Desire, by Deepak Chopra

Mindset: The New Psychology of Success. How we can Learn to Fulfill our Potential, by Carol S. Dweck PhD

Choose Yourself, by James Altucher

The Anticipation Map

Here are some great books to help you develop the right attitudes to face challenges:

The Marshmallow Test: Mastering Self-Control, by Walter Mischel

Flourish: A Visionary New Understanding of Happiness and Well-Being, by Martin E.P. Seligman

Learned Optimism: How to Change Your Mind and Your Life, by Martin E.P. Seligman

Gratitude, by Oliver Sacks

The Ritual Map

Here are some great books to learn about the power of habit and ritual:

The Power of Habit: Why We Do What We Do in Life and Business, by Charles Duhigg

Willpower: Rediscovering the Greatest Human Strength, by Roy F. Baumeister and John Tierney

The Willpower Instinct: How Self-Control Works, Why It Matters, and What You Can Do to Get More of It, by Kelly McGonigal

The Task Map

Here are some great books that deal with effective action and strategic planning:

Getting Things Done: The Art of Stress-Free Productivity, by David Allen

First Things First, by Stephen R. Covey, A. Roger Merrill, and Rebecca R. Merrill.

Essentialism: The Disciplined Pursuit of Less, by Greg McKeown

The One Thing: The Surprisingly Simple Truth Behind Extraordinary Results, by Gary Keller with Jay Papasan

The Power of Focus: How to Hit your Business, Personal and Financial Targets with Absolute Certainty, by Jack Canfield, Mark Victor Hansen, and Les Hewitt.

Eat That Frog! 21 Great Ways to Stop Procrastinating and Get More Done in Less Time, by Brian Tracy

General

Here are some classic success books that should be in any success seekers' library:

Think and Grow Rich, by Napoleon Hill

Seven Habits of Highly Effective People: Powerful Lessons in Personal Change, by Stephen R. Covey

The Success Principles: How to Get from Where You Are to Where You Want to Be, by Jack Canfield

Maximum Achievement: Strategies and Skills the will Unlock your Hidden Powers to Succeed, by Brian Tracy

ABOUT THE AUTHOR

Robert G. Allen's first book, the colossal #1 *New York Times* bestseller, *Nothing Down: How to Buy Real Estate with Little or No Money Down,* is the highest selling real estate investment book in history, and established "Bob" as one of the most influential investment advisors of all time.

In his following bestsellers, *Creating Wealth, The Challenge, Multiple Streams of Income,* and *The One Minute Millionaire* (with co-author Mark Victor Hansen), he expanded on his highly profitable techniques and philosophy. Today, there are thousands of millionaires who attribute their success partly to their contact with Bob.

He is a popular television and radio guest, appearing on hundreds of radio and television programs and podcasts. His books have over four million copies in print.

It is his purpose in life to help you achieve your dreams.

You can connect with him online at

www.robertallen.com